CELEBRATE THE
AMERICAN WAY

A Fun ESL Guide to English Language and Culture in the U.S.

Sheila MacKechnie Murtha, M.A.
Jane Airey O'Connor, M.Ed.

Research & Education Association
Visit our website at: www.rea.com

Research & Education Association
61 Ethel Road West
Piscataway, New Jersey 08854
E-mail: info@rea.com

**Celebrate the American Way: A Fun ESL Guide
to English Language and Culture in the U.S.**

Published 2017

Printed in the United States of America

Library of Congress Control Number 2015944894

ISBN-13: 978-0-7386-1194-5
ISBN-10: 0-7386-1194-8

Table of Contents

Winter

Spring

Summer

Autumn/Fall

Answers to Exercises

Appendices

About Our Authors

(Everything you wanted to know . . . and more!)

Sheila and Jane have been colleagues and friends for . . . well, let's just say a long time. ☺ As ESL (English as a Second Language) teachers, they have worked together on tons of projects . . . and they always had lots of fun as they worked. A partnership was born!

Together, Jane and Sheila have teaching credentials in several states and on two continents. With years and years… and years… of experience (they just don't want to count them all, ha!), they have taught ESL to little kids, big kids, university students, adult workers, company executives, and other teachers in the U.S. and Europe (both online and in regular classroom settings).

Both Sheila and Jane have served as members of the New Jersey Department of Education Advisory Committee for ESL/Bilingual Education. They've facilitated online ESL training courses for teachers through the NJ DOE professional development program. Sheila has held several leadership positions scoring English teacher candidate responses for an international testing company, and Jane has written ESL test questions and rated English as a Foreign Language exams for another internationally recognized testing company. (They teach! They test! They score!)

They've been recognized for excellence in teaching, and have won several awards, including two Teacher-of-the-Year awards, and corporate citations for excellence. They've given numerous presentations, and they've written curricula and syllabi for diverse ESL populations. Add to this some fun teaching projects in French, Spanish, public speaking, drama, writing. . . and, we're not kidding, even soccer skills (okay, not our finest moment) . . . and you've got two writers who know how to have a good time writing a book!

Jane is Director of ESL Services for Emory College of Arts and Sciences in Atlanta, Georgia.

Sheila is a Lecturer in the English Language Program at the University of Pennsylvania, and she continues to teach, write, and consult in New Jersey and New York.

They may live several states apart, but Sheila and Jane always find time to work together on FUN projects . . . like this book!

A Letter from the Authors

Hi there!

Thanks for choosing our book. We hope you'll love it!

As usual, we had lots of fun writing this book, and we hope you'll have lots of fun reading it. Well, have fun, but also learn interesting stuff about American culture, and why and how Americans celebrate important holidays. And while you're learning that, you'll learn tons of new vocabulary and idioms. As you learn about American customs and attitudes, you'll read (and hear!) plenty of informal English. REAL English!

We hope this book will be useful… and FUN!

Let's celebrate!

Sheila   Jane

Authors' Acknowledgments

Sheila says: Thanks to Erin, my one-woman cheering team, sounding board, culture consultant, and best friend; to James and Mak, always (quietly!) there for support and insider perspective; and Jimmy… always the voice in my head and my heart…

Jane says: Thanks to my wonderful husband Tony for doing no more than roll his eyes when I said Sheila and I were going to write another book. Thanks to my lovely daughter Charlotte (as she'll never forgive me if I don't mention her). And thanks to the bleachers at Swim Atlanta where a lot of this was written while Charlotte (see Charlotte I got your name in three times!) did her swim practice.

How This Book Works

The emphasis is on fun in this lighthearted guide to language and culture in the United States.

Celebrate the American Way takes you on a year-long journey through American social customs, highlighting the meanings behind the U.S. holidays and special events celebrated in each season. Learn why Americans mark Independence Day on July 4th, discover the history of Thanksgiving, get tips on wedding etiquette, find out how to carve a jack-o-lantern, and more!

Each section is chock-full of vocabulary and informal language related to the season or occasion. Wacky idioms, verbs, and slang expressions are shown in bold as they're introduced in the text and then listed at the end of each section with a simple definition or explanation.

Throughout the book, look for "Your Turn" practice exercises. Quiz yourself with these fun fill-in and matching activities as you learn about commonly confused words, adjectives, and synonyms. You'll find that these are great ways to check your understanding (and memory ☺).

Good luck, and have fun!

Symbols Used in the Book:

Look for this symbol (ⓘ) in the vocabulary lists to find idioms and other **informal language**, phrases, and slang. These common expressions are used in the U.S. by native English language speakers. Our definitions will help you understand the special meaning beyond the words so you'll never feel left out of a conversation.

"Just for Fun" gives you suggestions on enjoyable ways you can take part in the holidays and celebrate with others.

"Info to Know" sections tell you more about each holiday and explain seasonal events.

When you see this symbol, listen to the **audio track** to hear native speakers talk about the subject. Transcripts for each audio track can be found in Appendix A, which begins on page 197.

About REA

Founded in 1959, Research & Education Association (REA) is dedicated to publishing the finest and most effective educational materials—including study guides and test preps—for students of all ages.

Today, REA's wide-ranging catalog is a leading resource for students, teachers, and other professionals. Visit *www.rea.com* to see a complete listing of all our titles.

Acknowledgments

In addition to our authors, we would like to thank Pam Weston, Publisher, for setting the quality standards for production integrity and managing the publication to completion; Larry B. Kling, Vice President, Editorial, for his overall direction; Diane Goldschmidt, Managing Editor, for project management; and Eve Grinnell, Graphic Artist, for designing our cover and typesetting this edition.

WINTER

WINTER

♪ *LET IT SNOW, LET IT SNOW, LET IT SNOW!* ♪

Sure, we're singing it now . . . but just wait until the first snowstorm **dumps** 12 inches of **the white stuff**. Let's see who's singing that happy **tune** then. Ha! Yes, just as you finish raking the golden leaves of autumn, here comes Old Man Winter with another job for you to do: **shovel** the snow. It may mean some work, but there's something exciting about the first

"Hello, Old Man Winter and Jack Frost. Good morning, Mother Nature."

Ha, these aren't our neighbors—they're weather words!

Mother Nature rules *all* weather in *all* seasons. Old Man Winter is the **cranky** guy blowing icy winter winds. And Jack Frost? He painted those ice **designs** on your window!

We call it *personification* when we give human qualities to something not human . . . like the weather.

snowfall of the season. It's even better if it means a **snow day**! When kids hear the **snowplows** in the **middle of the night**, they **cross their fingers**, hoping that schools will be closed.

Guess what, kids. Your teachers are crossing their fingers, too. **No kidding!** Everybody loves a snow day! YAY! No school! No work! This is not a day to waste—kids **bundle up** and **head out** for **snowball fights**, building **snowmen** (hmm . . . or snow*women*, ha!) and making **snow angels**. Even the **grown-ups** go **sledding** and **ice skating**. Friends make **weekend plans** to **hit the slopes**—fresh snow is perfect for **skiing** and **snowboarding**. And when everyone is **freezing** and tired, there's no better way to end the day than with a **steaming mug** of **hot chocolate**! Enjoy it while you can, **folks**. Tomorrow the roads will be **clear**, and it's back to work for you!

We cold weather people have one word of advice about dressing for the cold: **LAYERS**!

This means to wear a light shirt, then another warmer shirt over it. Put a sweater over that, and then put on a warm coat. Layers!

Moms sometimes put so many warm layers on little kids that they look like little colorful **snowballs**, ready to roll down a hill! (Which is exactly what they want to do on a snowy day!)

Of course, not all parts of the United States are cold in winter (and our friends in Florida, in Arizona, and on the **West Coast** love to remind us of that!), but wherever you are, winter is a season that has **a lot going on**. It's the busiest holiday season of the year, with parties everywhere. There are family parties, office parties, class parties, neighborhood parties . . . you get the idea. That's a lot of party **refreshments**! Ha! Too many of those snacks and you'll be shopping for a bigger New Year's Eve **outfit**.

Yes, **chances are** you've decided on something extra-special to wear for New Year's Eve. It's an exciting night when lots of people get very **dressed up** for special parties. On this night it seems that everything sparkles: moonlight glistens on fresh snow; fancy clothes glitter in soft house lights; candles flicker in holiday windows; and, of course, champagne bubbles sparkle in crystal **flutes**. Cheers! Let the party begin!

And what a party it is! Everyone is happy to be with friends to "**ring in** the new year." As **midnight** gets close, champagne glasses are filled with **bubbly**, and people **gather** around a TV to watch the **ball drop**. (Ha! Or maybe they just want to watch the crazy **adventure-lovers** who are freezing in Times Square in New York City! *Brrr!*) The countdown begins at 60 seconds before midnight . . . until finally . . . 3 . . . 2 . . . 1 . . . . HAPPY NEW YEAR! Friends share kisses and drink a **toast** to a great new year. But let's see how many of them remember to write the new year date the next day. HA!

Of course, not everyone celebrates by going out to a party. Lots of people stay home and let the kids **stay up** late. At midnight, they may go outside to make lots of noise by hitting pots. Some people like to **set off fireworks** . . . BOOM! Some throw **streamers** and **pop party poppers**! Then, good-night, kids! Don't get up too early—we may need some extra sleep! Tomorrow will be Day One of trying to keep our New Year's **resolutions**. Typical resolutions are to **quit** smoking, or exercise more, or stop eating **junk food** and lose weight. And everybody *always* keeps *every* resolution!! . . . um . . . okay, for at least . . . a day . . . Hey! **It's the thought that counts!**

And good thoughts are what people share on the third Monday in January. This is a **federal holiday** to observe the birthday of Martin Luther King, Jr. We honor Dr. King for his work in using peaceful ways to get civil rights for all people. Civil rights make it against the law to treat people differently because of their color, religion, sex, or nationality. Many cities have a "Day of Service" in honor of MLK. People do **charity** projects or volunteer to help others in the community.

Speaking of charity projects . . . Here's one that will make you **shiver**!

Does snowy, cold weather make you want to go swimming? OF COURSE NOT! IT'S FREEZING! But that's exactly how some people **raise money** to help others. It's the Polar Bear **Plunge**! People in swimsuits run into icy water, while we watch—nice and warm, in our heavy winter coats.

It's all for fun to help the community. Get those polar bear people some hot chocolate!

We celebrate another **civic** holiday on the third Monday in February. It's Presidents' Day. "Which presidents?" you ask. Take out your **wallet**. Do you have a **single**? No, no, no, don't send it to us! Take a look at the **bill** . . . That's George Washington, our first president. (Hey, the number ONE president is on the ONE dollar bill!) Okay, do you have a **five**? Hello, Abraham Lincoln! (Well, he was the sixteenth president, but we don't have a sixteen dollar bill.) Both of these important presidents are honored on Presidents' Day. Happy February birthday, Washington and Lincoln!

Are you a sports fan? The beginning of February means only one thing to American football fans: Super Bowl Sunday! The Super Bowl is the National Football League **championship** game, and it's *hugely* popular! **Advertisers** pay millions of dollars for just a 30-second TV **commercial** during the game. And the commercials themselves are famously funny. Raise your hand if you like the commercials better than the game . . . (US! Yes, that's us! We watch the commercials, then take a **nap** when the game comes back on. Yes, we admit it: Sheila + Jane + football = zzzzzzzzzzzzz. Let the husbands watch the crazy game!) If you're not taking a nap, you may be at a Super Bowl party. These loud parties begin in the afternoon, and football fans have all the snacks ready to go: nachos and chips, chicken wings and chili, pretzels and pizza. It's the biggest game of the season, and there's lots of **yelling** and **cheering** as the teams score . . . or miss. At half-time, when the teams **take a break**, so do the fans as they watch the **half-time show**. Crazy Super Bowl Sunday . . . before Back-to-Work Monday, ha!

SUPER BOWL

Okay, we admit it: We're not football fans. So we figured out a little **secret**: If everybody is at a Super Bowl party watching the game, no one will be shopping! The stores will be empty! No crowds!

But here's the **catch**: If you go early, lots of people will be getting snacks to prepare in the afternoon. If you go later, people will be shopping for things they forgot. If you wait until game time, you'll be too tired to move! So, yeah, when the game starts no one will be shopping. Including you!

(And if the weather people say a snowstorm is coming, there won't be any milk or bread left anyway! We don't know why everyone buys milk and bread before a snowstorm . . . it's just one of those crazy American winter facts.)

Then, before you know it, all the holidays and exciting events are over, and the winter white and fun of snow start to get not-so-magical and not-so-fun! People are tired of cold, and slush, and icy roads, and shoveling snow, and more cold, and . . . well, you get the idea. Just in time! We have a **silly** day called **Groundhog** Day on February 2. The scientists can't always get weather **predictions** right, but on this day we let some big **rodents** tell us when winter will end! Places all over have special Groundhog Day ceremonies with their "official" groundhogs. Tradition says that if the groundhog comes out of his **burrow** and sees his shadow, spring will be late, and we'll have six more weeks of winter. NOOOOOO!!!!

GROUNDHOGS

Cities name their "official" weather-predicting groundhogs! Punxsutawney Phil is the star in Pennsylvania, and he's probably the most famous weather-predicting groundhog of all. (We think if you can spell *Punxsutawney* you should be able to figure out the weather without asking a rodent . . . ha!)

New York City (NYC) has Staten Island Chuck (though we don't want to think about what happened one year when the **mayor** dropped him), and Atlanta, Georgia, has General Beau Lee.

But our very favorite of all is Jimmy the Groundhog. In 2015, Jimmy the Groundhog BIT THE MAYOR'S EAR in Sun Prairie, Wisconsin!! HE BIT THE MAYOR'S EAR!!

Which is a good lesson: If mayors want to know the weather, they should ask a **meteorologist** instead of a groundhog. (That story makes us laugh every time we remember it.) Anyway, it's just for fun (unless you're the mayor of Sun Prairie, Wisconsin!).

TAKE A LOOK: Words that SHINE!

There's no brighter, shinier season than winter, so this is a perfect time to take a look at *light* words! These bright words can make any writing, um, shine. Put on your sunglasses and take a look at these **brilliant** words. And—BONUS!—they can be used as nouns OR verbs, so they'll . . . um . . . *brighten* twice as many sentences.

Ha! Make that *three times* as many sentences . . .

These light words sure are hard workers. You can make them adjectives, too! Just add the suffix *–ing*.

That's a beautiful sparkling ring!

beam (verb): to shine in a ray of light
*What a beautiful day! The sun **beamed** down through the window, and the cat slept happily in the sunbeam.*

beam (noun): the ray of light
*The cat slept in the warm **beam** of light.*

---

dazzle (verb): to shine so brightly your eyes hurt!
*Hoo boy! When you leave the dark movie theater, the sun outside will **dazzle** you.*

dazzle (noun): the bright light that hurts your eyes
*The **dazzle** of daylight surprised her when she left the theater.*

---

flash (verb): to shine in a quick and sudden way
*WOW! The lightning **flashed** across the sky. A storm is coming!*

flash (noun): the quick light
*A **flash** of lightning often means a storm is coming.*

---

flicker (verb): to shine quickly on and off
*The lamp **flickered**, and then went out. Time for a new light bulb.*

flicker (noun): the light that shines
*The **flicker** of the bulb reminded him to buy a new one.*

---

gleam (verb): to shine, as a reflection
*The beautiful silver bowl **gleamed** on the table.*

gleam (noun): the reflected light
*The **gleam** of the polished bowl was bright on the table.*

---

glimmer (verb): to shine in a weak way, on and off
*It was a foggy night, and the Statue of Liberty's light **glimmered** in the harbor.*

glimmer (noun): the weakly shining light
*In the harbor, a **glimmer** of light showed where to look for the Statue of Liberty.*

glisten (verb): to shine off something wet
*As he worked in the hot sun, his face **glistened** with sweat.*

glisten (noun): the shine that comes from something wet
*There was a **glisten** of sweat on his lip.*

---

glitter (verb): to shine in tiny lights that flash
*The ocean **glittered** in the bright sun.*

glitter (noun): the flash caused by tiny bits of light
*She sat on the beach, watching the **glitter** of sunlight on the waves.*

---

glow (verb): to shine like light caused by heat
*The fire **glowed**, and everyone sat around it with hot chocolate and cold hands.*

glow (noun): a shine or brightness caused by warmth
*Their faces had a warm **glow** as they sipped the hot chocolate.*

---

sparkle (verb): to shine in lots of small flashes of light
*The diamond **sparkled** in the light. . . . She was dazzled!*

sparkle (noun): the look of small light flashes
*The **sparkle** of the diamond made her smile.*

---

twinkle (verb): to shine in a strong, then weak way, then strong again!
*The moon is out and the stars are **twinkling** . . . It's a perfect night!*

twinkle (noun): a light that shines on and off
*The **twinkle** of winter lights reminded her of stars.*

Here's a "glitter" that you really DO NOT want. Maybe you've seen it. (If you have, you may still have some in your hair, ha!) Glitter is a pretty, shiny **decoration**, but it will drive you crazy.

We're talking about those teeny tiny pieces of shiny metal... or plastic... or whatever it is! You see it on some greeting cards in the store. (Don't touch the glitter! It will come home to live with you forever!)

Kids like to use glitter to decorate their projects. (Haha! Be careful on Mother's Day, Mom!) You can buy little **jars** of glitter at a crafts store. (But don't say we didn't warn you . . .)

YOUR TURN!

This is your chance to . . . come on—you know what's coming—it's your chance to . . . SHINE! We've made it a little easier for you—the shiny missing words are used as verbs. Can you find which word from the list below works best in these sentences? There may be more than one that fits. (You may need to change the form of the verbs, as we did in the example sentences above.) Answers are on page 173.

beam	glisten
dazzle	glitter
flash	glow
flicker	sparkle
gleam	twinkle
glimmer	

1. The jewels in the little girl's princess crown _____.

2. The sailors were happy to see the light _____from the lighthouse to guide them safely to shore.

3. It's tricky driving in the country at night. The car's headlights will _____a deer near the road.

4. We lost power in the snowstorm, so we ate dinner as candles _____ on the table.

5. I've polished the car until it _____!

6. A storm's coming! Lightning is _____ across the sky.

7. The flashlight is _____weakly; I think it needs new batteries.

8. The newlyweds were happy just watching the stars _____ in the sky!

9. New Year's Eve? I want my dress to _____ like gold!

10. The fire is _____, and so are the kids' faces!

11. The snowman is _____ in the early morning sun. Don't melt, Frosty!

WEATHER WORDS

When a snowstorm is coming, meteorologists (the weather people) are the stars of TV! It's their **big chance**! Everyone **tunes in** to see when the storm will **hit**, and how much snow to expect. It can be tricky to **figure out** what all the snowy weather words mean. Here are some of them:

- **a dusting:** a light covering of snow
- **a blanket of snow:** a thick covering that looks like . . . well, a blanket.
- **flurries:** scattered snow (just a little)
- **freezing rain:** rain that freezes as soon as it touches ground. This is dangerous and very slippery . . . STAY HOME!
- **snow showers:** short periods of snow
- **heavy snow:** several inches in less than 24 hours
- **accumulation:** how much snow is on the ground
- **significant accumulation:** a LOT of snow on the ground!
- **blizzard:** a dangerous snowstorm with very strong winds
- **whiteout conditions:** you can't see anything because of heavy blowing snow. STAY HOME!
- **snowdrift:** deep hill of snow made by blowing winds
- **taper off:** become weaker
- **wintry mix:** rain, sleet, and snow
- **sleet:** ice mixed with rain or snow
- **slush:** melting, wet, dirty snow. Ick!
- **black ice:** ice on the road that you can't see. STAY HOME!

◀ **Now listen to Audio Track 2**
(transcript on page 197)

VOCABULARY

- **adventure-lovers:** people who like to do exciting, sometimes crazy (!) things
- **advertisers:** companies who make commercials to sell products
- **a five:** a five dollar bill
- ⓘ **a lot going on:** many things all happening at the same time
- **ball drop:** a giant ball of glass and crystal that slowly goes down a pole to count down the seconds to midnight on New Year's Eve in New York City

- **big chance:** an unusual opportunity to become famous or successful at something
- **bill:** paper money
- **brilliant:** very, very, *very* bright! Also, very intelligent
- ⓘ **bubbly:** champagne
- **bundle up:** dress really, *really* warmly
- **burrow:** a little tunnel under the ground where some animals live
- **catch:** disadvantage; complication; something sounds like a good idea . . . except for one small problem
- **championship:** game that decides who is the best in the entire sport
- **chances are:** it's likely; probable
- **charity:** helping others who may not have important things they need; also, an organization that helps people in need
- **cheering:** showing very LOUD support for your team
- **civic:** about government
- **clear (roads):** clean of snow and ice; make clean
- **commercial:** an advertisement for a product. On TV during the Super Bowl, commercials try to be entertaining.
- **cranky:** easily annoyed and bothered by things; in a bad mood
- ⓘ **cross your fingers:** hope that something happens
- **decoration:** a colorful thing to make something look pretty
- **designs:** patterns
- **dressed up:** wearing fancy clothes
- ⓘ **dump:** used often with snow to mean that a storm left a lot of snow on the ground! ("The snowstorm dumped twelve inches on the city!")
- **federal holiday:** an official government holiday; also, national holiday
- **figure out:** try to learn what something means
- **fireworks:** small explosives to make colorful displays of sparks in the sky
- **flute:** a tall crystal glass with a tall narrow container part for holding champagne
- **folks:** people
- **freezing:** feeling really, really, *really* cold! Also, a temperature below 32 degrees Fahrenheit.
- **gather:** bring together in a group
- **glitter:** the shiny sparkles on cards or little kids' projects
- **groundhog:** a rodent, about the size of a really fat cat
- **grown-ups:** adults

- **half-time show:** an exciting performance between two halves of a football game
- ⓘ **head out:** go someplace
- **hit:** arrive, as a big storm; also ⓘ go somewhere (hit the mall)
- ⓘ **hit the slopes:** go skiing in the mountains
- **hot chocolate:** come on, you know this! That yummy hot beverage of hot milk and chocolate!
- **ice skating:** wearing special shoelike boots with blades to slide across the ice
- ⓘ **it's the thought that counts:** even if the event is not successful, at least someone tried!
- **jar:** small glass container
- **junk food:** all the stuff you love to eat that is NOT good for you! (candy, cookies, donuts, chips, cheeseburgers . . . YUM!)
- ⓘ **kidding:** joking; not serious; fooling someone in a fun way
     are you kidding?!: What you just said sounds crazy to me!
     no kidding!: I mean it! Really, it's true!
     you're kidding!: expresses surprise at what someone just told you
     you're not kidding!: expresses excited agreement
- **layers:** items on top of items on top of items!
- **mayor:** an elected official in local government who leads a city
- **meteorologists:** people who analyze weather conditions
- **middle of the night:** usually from midnight to about 3AM
- **midnight:** 12:00AM (when we should all be asleep!)
- **mug:** a large, heavy cup for hot beverages
- ⓘ **nap:** a short sleep (often on the couch . . . hmm, I think I'll take a nap right now!)
- **outfit:** a set of clothes
- **party popper:** small plastic object, pull the string, hear the pop, and out comes a lot of small **streamers**. FUN!
- **plunge:** jump into water
- **pop:** to make a very small explosion; also, a sound . . . say it and you'll hear it!
- **predictions:** saying what will happen in the future
- **quit:** stop doing something
- **raise money:** collect donations for a charity
- **refreshments:** food and drinks
- **resolutions:** plans to make changes in order to become better or healthier people

- **ring in:** welcome with lots of noise
- **rodent:** animals with sharp teeth; for example, rats, mice, and GROUNDHOGS!
- **secret:** some information that no one else knows. *Shhh!*
- **set off:** light with a match to cause fireworks to explode
- **shiver:** shaking because of cold
- **shovel:** move snow (or something else); also the tool to move it
- ⓘ **silly:** not serious; kind of funny
- **single:** one dollar bill
- **skiing:** going down a snowy hill with long, thin slats on your feet!
- **sledding:** going down a snowy hill on a sled
- **snow angel:** an angel shape made by lying in the snow and moving arms up and down and legs back and forth
- **snowball:** a handful of snow squeezed into a ball shape . . . and thrown at friends for fun!
- **snowball fight:** friends throwing snowballs at each other in fun!
- **snowboarding:** going down a snowy hill standing on a board. *AAACKKK!!!*
- **snow day:** SNOW! NO SCHOOL!
- **snowfall:** amount of snow falling during a specific time
- **snowman:** a figure made from large amounts of snow
- **snowplow:** a truck with a special tool to clear snow from a road
- **stay up:** not go to bed at the usual time
- **steaming:** giving off steam, or vapor from heat
- **streamers:** long pieces of colorful paper
- ⓘ **take a break:** rest while doing some work
- ⓘ **the white stuff:** SNOW!
- **toast:** express good wishes while holding a glass of champagne; also, that nice crisp cooked piece of bread we love for breakfast.
- **tune:** a melody; musical sounds
- ⓘ **tunes in:** listens or watches on media
- **wallet:** a small folder for holding money, credit cards, and other things you want to carry
- **weekend plans:** activities you decide to do on Saturday and Sunday
- **West Coast:** the California part of the country! Also Oregon and Washington ☺
- **yelling:** speaking in a very, VERY LOUD VOICE!

CHRISTMAS

This is a **big** one! Not everyone celebrates Christmas, but it's the busiest American holiday of the year. For Christians, December 25 is a celebration of the birth of Christ. You'll know the holiday is coming just by taking a walk around the neighborhood! People **decorate** their homes with twinkling lights and flickering candles in the windows. Pretty **wreaths** of green branches, red berries, and **pine cones** are tied with glittering **ribbon** and hung on the front door. Inside, tables are decorated with **poinsettias** and pine **boughs** and **holly**. And sometimes you may find a ball of **mistletoe** hanging from a kitchen doorway. Ha! Be careful! Tradition says that if you meet someone under the mistletoe, you must kiss him (or her). STEP AWAY from the mistletoe!

Some people get *really* excited about decorating. Every year their decorations get brighter and crazier, with **giant** snowmen, reindeer, and **inflatable** Santas. Some neighborhoods have a contest (with prizes!) for the best decorations.

Some houses are trimmed with tons of lights, flashing on and off, or changing colors. Yikes! All those lights! All that electricity! The electric bills must be . . . **shocking**! (Haha, get it? Electric? . . . Shocking?!) We're glad *we* don't have to pay that electric bill!

Families all have their own ways of decorating their houses, but the most important part of all is **trimming** the Christmas tree. Lots of people choose a freshly cut **evergreen** because of the wonderful smell. But when those **needles** fall off, it's time to get out the **vacuum** . . . again . . . and again . . . and again . . . and . . . Trust us. No matter how many times you vacuum, you'll still find needles in July. (Ooh! Christmas in July!) Other people prefer an **artificial** tree—there are no needles to vacuum and they can use the same tree each year.

Trimming the tree is an exciting event for the family. **Tinsel** sparkles in the light. Shiny glass colored balls gleam next to **handmade ornaments**. Dad hangs **strings of lights** that twinkle—clear or in colors.

Kids hang **candy canes** and their favorite ornaments. Of course, Mom's favorites are the little decorations the kids have made, and she has saved, for years . . . and years . . . and years. And then, when the tree has no room for another ornament, it's time to **top it off** with a twinkling star or a beautiful angel.

Many houses have a **nativity** scene to represent the story of how simply Jesus was born, in a **stable**. A brightly shining star above the stable showed the **shepherds** and three visiting kings where to find him. Some churches may even have "living nativities" with people **dressed up** to act out the story.

For many little kids, the holiday is all about Santa Claus. Come on, you know the guy— long white **beard** . . . big red suit . . . kind of, um, **chubby**. Ho! Ho! Ho! Santa keeps a list, and he brings **presents** to children who have been good. If they've been **naughty**, he'll fill their **stockings** with **coal**. How does Santa do this, you may ask. HA–MAGIC! He flies from his home at the North Pole in a **sleigh** filled with toys. The sleigh is pulled by eight **reindeer**, and a very special leader: Rudolph the red-nosed reindeer!

In the weeks before Christmas, kids write letters to tell Santa what they're wishing for. Some make sure he gets the message by visiting him at the mall with their families. Have you seen these families? The babies are crying; the littlest kids are scared; the older ones are sitting **shyly** on Santa's lap **whispering** their wishes; the oldest kids are saying, "We are too cool to believe in Santa Claus" . . . and Mom and Dad are click, click, clicking away to get photos! We're not sure how Santa **pulls off** the trick of being in malls all over America at the same time, but we guess it's just more magic. Have you seen him at your **nearby** mall? You'll certainly see pictures of him everywhere. And you'll hear about him in the malls . . . Christmas **carols** play **endlessly**! You'll know them all **by heart** before long! Well, that is, unless you **avoid** the malls completely . . . which is not a bad idea if you can pull it off . . . because the malls are **mobbed** with

crowds of shoppers. Everyone wants to find the perfect **gift**, so they're at the mall, **checking off** their **Christmas lists**. Ha! Everyone except us. We're home on the sofa, shopping online.

Kids aren't the only ones writing at Christmas! E-mail, texting, social media . . . So far, they haven't **taken the place** of another holiday tradition: sending Christmas cards.

These are **greetings** to people we may not see often, wishing them happy holidays and good things for the new year. Families often send a picture of the kiddies. Some people send a "Christmas letter" telling about all the things that have happened in their family during the year.

Thanks, Uncle Fred! We're happy to know you finally figured out how to catch the N Train to Brooklyn! That really is a Christmas miracle!

(We can guarantee that you'll receive at least one card from someone you forgot. If you're lucky, it will come a few days before Christmas so you have time to send one back!)

And before you can say "**jingle bells**," the Big Day arrives. Before they go to bed on Christmas **Eve**, kids hang a stocking by the fireplace (or in another special place) for Santa to fill with **treats**. We hate to tell you this, Mom and Dad, but those kids will be too excited to sleep. You can expect them to come running at the **crack of dawn**: "Mom! Dad! WAKE UP! Santa was here! Come see the presents under the tree! . . . *LOOK!* Santa ate the cookies!" Yes, before they go to bed, kids leave cookies and milk for Santa. Hmm. I guess that explains his big **belly**. All those kids + cookies for Santa = well . . . a LOT of cookies!

Hey, speaking of cookies . . . There's another typical activity during the holiday season: Christmas baking. There are family favorites that people look forward to every year, like Aunt Rox's butter cookies with **pecans**, or Aunt Deb's yummy **brownies**. Nana is the Queen of **date** and nut bread, and Aunt Mell makes the best **quinoa kale oatmeal crunchies** in town! Of course, half the fun of baking is stealing a few treats, but last year Aunt Dawn was ready with her camera to take pictures of any **culprits**! Noooo!!!!!

When the baking is done, the decorations are up, the cards have been mailed, and the shopping is finished, the family **settles in** to watch holiday movies—the same ones again and again; year after year . . . it's a tradition! (When Charles Dickens wrote *A Christmas Carol* in 1843, we're pretty sure he never imagined that it would be a **classic** holiday movie today!) The movie themes are **heartwarming**, and spending **family time** is the nicest part of the holidays.

Want to see the most popular holiday movies? Here are our favorites. Somebody make the popcorn!

Old Classics:

- *It's a Wonderful Life*
- *A Christmas Carol*
- *Miracle on 34th Street*

Fun for Everyone:

- *A Christmas Story*
- *Home Alone*
- *Elf*
- *Christmas Vacation* (watch for our favorite actor: Keith MacKechnie!)

Animated Films:

- *Dr. Seuss's How the Grinch Stole Christmas*
- *The Muppet Christmas Carol*
- *A Charlie Brown Christmas*
- *The Polar Express*

◀ **Now listen to Audio Track 3**
(transcript on page 199)

TAKE A LOOK: Set Phrases With Light Words

A *set phrase* is a group of words commonly used together to show a special meaning. In these expressions, other words just wouldn't sound right to native speakers. Take a look at these shiny *light* words in their special expressions. You'll see them used this way a lot!

beam: to beam with pride—to be very happy about something
*The athlete **beamed with pride** as he accepted his award.*

dazzle: a dazzling smile—a really, *really* bright smile
*The toothpaste company promised, "No tooth problems, and a **dazzling smile!**"*

flash: to flash with anger—to quickly show an expression of anger
*Her eyes **flashed with anger** when her boss said, "This project is too complicated for you."*

flicker: a flicker of a frown—a quick expression of unhappiness or disappointment about something

*A **flicker of a frown** passed across her face when she found out she didn't get the promotion . . . but she was happy for her coworker who got the job.*

gleam: a gleam in his eye—a look of happiness or playfulness

*He had a **gleam in his eye** when he played his April Fool's trick.*

glimmer: a glimmer of hope—a small chance that something good will happen

*There wasn't a **glimmer of hope** that she would pass the exam—she hadn't studied anything!*

glisten: glisten with tears—shine with happy or sad tears

*As she watched the sad movie, her eyes **glistened with tears**.*

glitter: a glittering occasion—a very fancy occasion

*We love watching the Academy Awards! It's always a **glittering occasion** full of movie stars and beautiful clothes.*

glow: in glowing terms—using words of praise

*The principal spoke about the hard-working student **in glowing terms**.*

sparkle: sparkling wit—bright and funny sense of humor

*She was a very popular speaker because of her **sparkling wit**.*

twinkle: a twinkle in his eye—a look of playfulness

*The little boy had a **twinkle in his eye** just before he pulled on Santa's beard! That beard was real!*

YOUR TURN!

How brightly can YOU shine? Can you choose the best set phrases from the list above for these sentences? Some may be used in more than one place. Go on, dazzle us! Answers are on page 173.

1. The new mother _____ as she looked at her baby's face.

2. When he saw Santa at the mall, the little boy's face lit up with a _____ _____!

3. Santa looked at the little boy and, with a _____, asked, "Have you been a good boy?"

4. They were excited to attend the New Year's Eve party! It was always a _____, with special food, beautiful lights, and guests in fancy clothes.

5. Her eyes _____ when her child said, "I love you, Mom."

6. Uncle Fred's Christmas letter told, _____, how fabulous the NYC subway system is!

7. When she learned that someone had stolen some of the Polar Bear Plunge donations, her eyes _____.

8. She still had a _____ that the money would be returned.

9. A _____ passed across her face when she couldn't find her favorite tree ornament.

10. He was always popular at parties! People enjoyed his _____ and funny stories.

☑ CHRISTMAS INFO TO KNOW:

☑ Christmas is a huge holiday across the United States, but, of course, not every American celebrates it. You will probably hear many people say the traditional greeting, "Merry Christmas!" when they meet around the holidays. The meaning of this is simply to share the joy of the holidays. But because there are so many different holidays around this time, with so many different ethnic and religious celebrations, more people prefer to say, "Happy Holidays!" This is a way to share good wishes with everyone, no matter what winter holiday they celebrate!

The expression "Merry Christmas" goes back hundreds of years, but you may never hear the word *merry* except around the holidays! It means *joyful* and *very happy*, but it's not a word used often in everyday American English.

Another expression sometimes used around the holidays in a fun, joking way is "Bah! Humbug!" It's a way to say, "None of this holiday stuff for me!"

Dickens's character, the **mean** Mr. Scrooge, was serious when he said it, but if you hear "Bah! Humbug!" there's probably a big smile right behind it!

 You may be invited to a "Holiday Cookie Exchange." This is a fun (and delicious!) way to get fabulous recipes. Bring a **batch** of your favorite holiday cookies and copies of the recipe. Bring enough to share! You'll get to taste lots of cookies and collect yummy new recipes.

 A group of coworkers may want to exchange Christmas or holiday gifts, but this can be expensive. A popular tradition among friends is to have "Secret Santa." Here's how it works: Everyone's name is written on a piece of paper. Without **peeking**, each friend **picks** a name. That's the person you'll buy a gift for. *Shhh!* Don't tell your friend! The group will decide how much money may be spent on the gift. Everyone keeps it a secret until gifts are exchanged, usually at a holiday party. Your Secret Santa will be **revealed**! Are you surprised? Did you think it was someone else?

Secret Santa is a really popular tradition in large families, too. Selecting just one person to buy a gift for makes it easier to think about "the perfect gift" for just that one person.

Some people call this tradition "Kris Kringle" or "Pollyanna."

Some groups at work add another fun part to the tradition. In the weeks leading up to Christmas, a person will surprise her Secret Santa friend with little treats: candy on her desk one day, maybe a small plant another day, just a happy note another day. But *shhh!* Don't let her know they're from you! That's a secret until the last day!

 Sometimes other close friends may exchange small gifts. These are usually things like baked goods—homemade cookies are a favorite! Or someone might give a special coffee mug and a small package of special coffee or tea. These are often given in a holiday decorated bag, or they are covered in clear wrap and tied with a colorful ribbon. Happy Holidays!

Charles Dickens gave us "Bah! Humbug!" in *A Christmas Carol*. But in another book, he wrote the line that perfectly describes visiting New York City around the holidays . . . "It was the best of times, it was the worst of times . . . "

Yes, New York City, Philadelphia, and Washington, D.C., are winter wonderlands of twinkling lights, sparkling decorations, glistening snow, and the rosy glow of people's pink cheeks in the **bitter cold**.

Sounds perfect, doesn't it? IT IS! We LOVE NYC at the holidays! But, guess what. So do millions of other people. **Come on**, you know what that means . . . It means . . . CROWDS! It means LINES! It means NO TAXIS!

Everyone wants to experience the magic of winter holidays in New York City and other big, cold cities . . . (WHAT?! We can hear you, California!)

Just **keep in mind**: every place you want to go, every Broadway show you want to see, every place you want to shop, and every street you need to travel will be . . . **CROWDED**!

See what we mean? "The best of times, the worst of times . . . "

Happy Holidays!

◀ **Now listen to Audio Track 4**
(transcript on page 200)

YOUR TURN!

You've probably seen these **symbols** of Christmas. (If you haven't, you will!) Can you match the words to the pictures? Answers are on page 173.

1. _____ mistletoe
2. _____ candle
3. _____ stocking
4. _____ ornament
5. _____ fire

6. _____ holly
7. _____ wreath
8. _____ sleigh
9. _____ present
10. _____ Christmas tree
11. _____ snowman
12. _____ tree light

Hey, Christmas shopping may be over, but that doesn't mean fun at the mall is over. Nooooo! Now it's time for **RETURNS**!

Did you know that you can bring things back to the store if you change your mind about them? Well, you need to know about "holiday returns"! Americans LOVE holiday shopping, but there's another shopping activity that's just as busy: returning all that stuff for a **refund** or **exchange**!

Is the sweater you got for your sister the wrong size? Exchange it for another size! Does Uncle Fred already have the subway book you gave him? Return it! Did you get two red hats? Exchange one for a different color. Or return one!

On the day after Christmas, stores are crowded again—this time with people exchanging or returning their gift **purchases**. Stores in the U.S. make it easy for people to return items that have not been used. Usually you just need your purchase **receipt**.

Don't have a receipt? You can often return a gift someone gave you—a "gift return"—without a receipt. The store will exchange it for something else, or give you a **store credit**.

But there's a time limit, which can be from two weeks to a month. For holiday purchases, stores usually allow more time so that gifts can be returned into January.

We know you'll love your holiday gifts, but if you don't . . . RETURN THEM!

◀ **Now listen to Audio Track 5**
(transcript on page 202)

FUN WITH IDIOMATIC EXPRESSIONS: It's cold!

Hey, California! You may not believe it, but we really do love the snowy part of winter! Lots of people hope for a "white Christmas" to make the holidays extra special. It may be cold, but it sure is pretty! Here are some fun (and very chilly!) idioms.

- **snowed in:** trapped! You can't leave a place because the snow is too deep
  *They watched movies, played games, and ate lots of snacks. Hey, it's FUN to be **snowed in**!*

- **snowed under:** overworked; having a **TON** of things to do
  *Sorry, I can't go to the party tonight. I'm **snowed under** with work I need to finish. Hey, it's NOT FUN to be **snowed under**!*

- **break the ice:** stop the uncomfortable feeling people have with a new group; do something to make strangers begin talking
  *Alfredo really knows how to **break the ice** with a new group of students—he tells his wacky funny jokes and everyone starts to laugh and talk.*

- **skating on thin ice:** doing something that could be a problem
  *Yufei was **skating on thin ice** when she told her boss she thought the project was boring.*

- **get cold feet:** become nervous about something you had planned to do and change your mind
  *She told her friends she'd meet them on the ski slope, but when she saw how high the mountain was, she **got cold feet** and sat in the lodge. (Ha! She **got cold feet** . . . then she got hot chocolate!)*

 JUST FOR FUN!

 It may be freezing and snowy, but that doesn't mean you can't **pretend** it's spring! Check your town or a nearby city for a Flower Show. The New York Botanical Garden always has beautiful displays, even in the **dead of winter**. Every year, the Philadelphia Horticultural Society presents the Philadelphia Flower Show. Our favorite orchid **extravaganza** happens in February. Orchids and flowers and beautiful spring plants in February . . . Snowstorm? What snowstorm?!

Build a house! WHAT?! Haha—Do you think we're crazy? We're not kidding! Have you heard the expression "dream house"? It means the house you wish you could have. Well, the holidays are a perfect time to build *our* idea of the perfect "dream house"—one that you can EAT! HA!

Because we like things fun and easy, here's our suggestion for building a traditional gingerbread house: Buy a **kit**! It will have the cookie walls and roof pieces (the hard parts!) already made. You just put the pieces together with **icing** "**glue**," and decorate with candy! (Hint: We've even done this using graham crackers.) And if that's too much work, you can even find houses ALREADY completely made . . . just decorate! Did you guess that our favorite part is getting all the candy together? Ha! Don't eat the decorations before you make the house!

VOCABULARY

- **artificial:** not natural; made by machine
- **avoid:** stay away from
- **batch:** a large amount of something made at one time
- **beard:** the hair a guy has on his chin. Santa has a big white beard!
- ⓘ **belly:** stomach
- ⓘ **big:** very popular
- **bitter cold:** a set phrase to describe *extremely* cold weather
- **boughs:** small branches of a tree
- **brownies:** sweet, chocolate, cakelike baked treats
- ⓘ **by heart:** to know something perfectly
- **candy canes:** striped peppermint candies in a cane shape; usually red and white
- **carol:** a Christmas song
- **checking off:** putting a mark to show you finished that item
- **Christmas list:** the names of people you are shopping for, and ideas for what gifts to buy
- ⓘ **chubby:** umm, a little, umm, overweight
- **classic:** something that everyone agrees is excellent

- **coal:** carbon-based stuff that used to be used commonly in the United States for fuel
- ⓘ **come on:** Tell the truth! also, you know it's true! also, hurry up!
- ⓘ **crack of dawn:** the very earliest time of the morning. Please! Let me go back to sleep!
- **crowd:** LOTS of people. *Aaaackkk!!!*
- **crowded:** filled with TOO many people!
- **crunchies:** treats that are, well, crunchy
- **culprits:** people doing things they shouldn't be doing. (Like stealing a cookie!)
- **date:** a small dried fruit from a palm tree; delicious in a sweet bread
- **dead of winter:** the middle of the winter with cold winter weather
- **decorate:** make something more beautiful for example with lights and balloons
- **dressed up:** in a costume to play an acting part; also, wearing fancy clothes
- **endlessly:** forever! again and again and again and *again* and . . . you get the idea
- **eve:** the night before, as in Christmas Eve or New Year's Eve
- **evergreens:** trees, like pines, that stay green all winter
- **exchange:** trade for something else
- **extravaganza:** a really, really, *really* exciting event!
- **family time:** time spent together doing fun things
- **giant:** really, really, *really* big
- **gift:** see *present*
- **glue:** sticky stuff that joins objects together
- **greetings:** messages of good wishes for an occasion
- **handmade:** made one piece at a time by a person
- **heartwarming:** making people feel emotionally happy
- **holly:** a dark green plant with red and white berries; very popular in Christmas decorations
- **icing:** very sweet cream that goes on top of cakes and cookies; also known as *frosting.* YUM!
- **inflatable:** something that becomes really big when you blow air into it
- **jingle bells:** the sound of winter bells . . . and a song you'll hear for weeks during the holiday season!
- **kale:** a green leafy, healthful vegetable that, in our opinion, should only be eaten by rabbits, not people!

- **keep in mind:** remember
- **kit:** a container that has all the items you need to complete a project
- **mean:** unkind; not nice; not generous (like Mr. Scrooge in *A Christmas Carol*)
- **mistletoe:** a grayish green plant that has white berries in winter
- ⓘ **mobbed:** very, very, *very* crowded
- **nativity:** about the birth of Jesus Christ
- **naughty:** misbehaving; not being good, especially a kid
- **nearby:** not far; close
- **needle:** the very sharp, small leaf of an evergreen tree
- **oatmeal:** grain for cereal (we like it for breakfast)
- **ornaments:** special items used to decorate, or make something look pretty
- **pecans:** nuts from a hard shell, often used in baking
- ⓘ **peek:** look at something secretly
- **picks:** choose, select
- **pine cone:** the long, round-ish woody seed holder of a pine tree
- **poinsettia:** beautiful red plant commonly seen around Christmas time; grown commonly in Mexico
- **present:** gift; something nice you give to someone for a special occasion
- **pretend:** act as if something is so when it isn't!
- ⓘ **pull (something) off:** be able to do something very tricky!
- **purchase:** to buy; also something that someone has bought
- **quinoa:** a tiny healthful grain
- **receipt:** copy of payment that shows what you bought and when you bought it
- **refund:** get (or give) money back after a purchase
- **reindeer:** a type of deer with antlers (horns); usually found in cold regions
- **returns:** purchases or gifts brought back to the store
- **reveal:** show
- **ribbon:** a long, very narrow piece of fabric used for decoration, and to tie on gifts
- ⓘ **settle in:** get comfortable after doing other things
- **shepherd:** someone who takes care of sheep
- **shocking:** very surprising in a bad way; also the feeling when electricity goes through a body

- **shyly:** in a timid, quiet way
- **sleigh:** a large open sled, with room for someone to sit and carry things
- **stable:** a simple wooden structure for keeping animals
- **stocking:** a special, very large sock designed especially for Christmas treats
- **store credit:** a card allowing someone to spend money but only in a specific store
- **string of lights:** many lights on a single electrical wire, used for decorating
- **symbol:** a sign or object used to represent something else
- ⓘ **take the place of something:** replace; do or use a new thing instead of the original item
- **tinsel:** thin, silvery decoration
- **ton:** a *LOT*
- ⓘ **top it off:** finish decorating with something on top
- **treats:** sweet foods, like cookies and candy, that we shouldn't eat very often. (But we do, haha!)
- **trimming:** decorating
- **vacuum:** clean with a vacuum!
- **whispering:** speaking in a very, very soft voice
- **wreath:** a circle decoration made of twigs, leaves, and other decorations, usually hung on a door at Christmas

HOLIDAYS OF LIGHT!
HANUKKAH, KWANZAA, AND CHINESE NEW YEAR

HANUKKAH

You've probably noticed that *light* is, um . . . *shining* through this entire season. For Jewish people, Hanukkah is a **joyous** eight-day holiday of light that's usually celebrated in December (it follows the lunar calendar). In fact, it's often called a *Festival of Lights*, and its symbol is a special candle holder called a **menorah**. For each of the eight nights of Hanukkah, Jewish families look forward to the tradition of lighting one candle on the menorah, until they are all lit at the end of the holiday. During the days of Hanukkah, people exchange gifts, and children play special games. Kids **spin** a traditional toy called a **dreidel** . . . The winner gets small treats. YAY, treats! And of course there are traditional foods—our favorites are the **latkes** (delicious fried potato pancakes) and, of course, the jelly donuts . . . (Oh, the *jelly donuts*!!!) Children love getting **gelt** from family members . . . Of course they do! These are chocolate "**coins**" **wrapped** in shiny gold paper. Traditional foods! Chocolate! Candles and light! Happy Hanukkah!

KWANZAA

Wait! Did you think we've **covered** all the December holidays with candles and light? No! Another holiday that is celebrated by many African Americans is Kwanzaa. This holiday was created in the 1960s as a way to bring African American people together in celebrating their culture. Kwanzaa begins on December 26 and lasts for seven days. On each day people light a candle and talk about a special Kwanzaa "**principle**." These seven principles honor the ideas of becoming better people and communities, and helping one another. Some people wear traditional African clothes, and some celebrate with songs and dances. Many of these customs are based on the **harvest** celebrations in Africa. On the last day of Kwanzaa, people exchange gifts and enjoy an African feast.

CHINESE NEW YEAR

This is one of our favorites! If you're lucky enough to live in or near a place with a large **population** of Asian Americans, you'll be able to experience a fabulous and exciting celebration of the Chinese New Year! This winter holiday, also called the Spring Festival, occurs in late January or early February. It's **LOUD**! It's COLORFUL! It's DELICIOUS! The celebration usually begins with a huge fireworks show. Tradition says that this will keep away bad spirits . . . and we believe it! Those **firecrackers** are loud! We love watching the **parade** . . . along with the huge crowds of people . . . but our favorite parts are the colorful and exciting lion and dragon dances.

The date for Chinese New Year changes because the Asian calendar goes by the moon. In fact, this holiday is also called Lunar New Year. (Lunar means "relating to the moon.")

Whatever we call it, we LOVE this celebration!

There's something for everyone at the Chinese New Year festival! Flower markets are a popular tradition, and, of course, special foods and treats are everywhere! In New York City, the streets of Chinatown are filled with **vendors** selling **crafts** and yummy foods like **dumplings**. (Someone told us that eating lots of dumplings is lucky and means we'll become **rich** during the year. If that's true, then we will be very, *very* rich because we eat lots and lots of dumplings! . . . . *urp* . . .) Someone also told us that San Francisco is the place to be if you really want to experience the Spring Festival/Chinese New Year/Lunar New Year in the U.S.! (We're not sure about that—we really love our NYC Chinatown celebration!)

San Francisco has one of the largest and most exciting Chinese New Year parades in the world! IN THE WORLD! It's huge! Hundreds of thousands of people watch this parade—**in person** or on TV.

We can't be in San Francisco for the celebration this year, but it's on our list of Things To Do!

Lots of big cities have a Chinatown . . . a neighborhood with a very large number of Chinese people. It's the place to go for REAL Chinese cultural items and food.

We love all the streets and shops around Canal Street in New York City's Chinatown. We're not sure what all those vegetables are, and we've never seen some of those fish before, but we're sure they'll be delicious!

Another spot we love is the Friendship Gate in Philadelphia. It's right at the entrance to the Chinatown neighborhood. The Friendship Gate is a symbol of . . . yes, friendship (!), and cultural exchange between Philadelphia and a city in China. In fact, **craftspeople** from that city came to Philadelphia to create the gate.

You can't miss the beautiful bright colors and designs welcoming you to this cultural section of town.

Welcome to Chinatown!

In Chinese tradition, the color red symbolizes good luck, **wealth**, and happiness, so you'll see it in lots of cards and decorations. In Chinese American homes, adults give children red envelopes with money. Save it, kids! Houses that were cleaned **top to bottom** before the holiday are decorated with lots of traditional symbols: There are paper **lanterns**, Chinese writings, flowers, bowls of oranges, and the color red everywhere. We don't speak Chinese, but we DO speak Chinese celebration, so "Best wishes for a happy and prosperous New Year!" Or, as our celebrating friend Yu-Ching tells us, we can say: *Gung hay fat choy!*

TAKE A LOOK: *-ed* and *-ing* adjectives

One of the really tricky things to **get the hang of** in English is using adjectives that end in *-ed* or *-ing*. Is the Chinese New Year parade *excited*? Or is it *exciting*? Are you *bored*? Or are you *boring*? (Haha! We hope you're neither!)

There are lots of adjectives that can end in *-ed* or *-ing*, but how do you know which one to use? Think of it this way: If it ends in *-ed*, it generally describes how someone *feels*. If it ends in *-ing*, it describes the situation that *makes* someone feel *-ed*! It's almost like cause and effect: If it's *-ing*, then it will cause someone to feel *-ed*. Get it? Look at these examples:

- **The student** was *bored* because **the class** was *boring*. (YAWN! The student *felt* bored because the class was boring. It was not an interesting class because the teacher just talked and talked, and the students just wrote and wrote.)
- **The kids** were *excited* because **the parade** was *exciting*. (The kids *felt* excited because the parade was exciting, with dancing and costumes and loud music, and it made the kids feel that way.)

Here are some more:

You feel . . .	. . . because something is. . .	You feel . . .	. . . because something is. . .
amused	amusing	excited	exciting
annoyed	annoying	frightened	frightening
confused	confusing	frustrated	frustrating
disappointed	disappointing	interested	interesting
embarrassed	embarrassing	satisfied	satisfying
encouraged	encouraging	surprised	surprising
entertained	entertaining	tired	tiring

YOUR TURN!

Is it *-ed* or is it *-ing*? This is challeng*ing*! Are you feeling challeng*ed*? Decide which adjective fits best, and circle it in the sentences below. Answers are on page 174.

1. We like learning about how different people celebrate different holidays! It's very ***interested/interesting*** to compare cultures.

2. Holidays are always fun, but they can be very ***tired/tiring*** . . . or is that just us (zzzzzzzz)?

3. Everyone was ***excited/exciting*** by the music and fun of the Lion Dance!

4. With the kids spinning dreidels and hoping for treats, Hanukkah games are really ***amused/amusing***.

5. The little boy was afraid Santa knew he pulled his sister's hair. But he was ***encouraged/encouraging*** when Santa said, "I know you've been very good!"

6. BOO! Everyone was ***disappointed/disappointing*** when the groundhog saw his shadow. Six more weeks of winter? BOO!

7. She was really ***surprised/surprising*** when she found out the boss was her Secret Santa!

8. Mom thought it would be fun to bring the baby to see Santa at the mall. WRONG! The baby started crying like crazy! She was ***frightened/frightening*** by that big hairy guy in the red suit!

9. Kwanzaa is a ***satisfied/satisfying*** time for African Americans, as they honor African traditions and principles of respect and community.

10. The driver was ***confused/confusing*** when the street he wanted was closed for the Chinese New Year parade. (Recalculate, Siri!)

WINKER HOLIDAY INFO TO KNOW:

 Office parties are very common around the holidays, and they can be a really fun time to enjoy celebrating with coworkers. Everyone enjoys the holiday decorations for *all* the holidays: snowflakes, Christmas trees, African candles, menorahs, and Chinese symbols. But most importantly, people enjoy a very casual, fun time with coworkers and their, ***ahem***, bosses. It's fun to celebrate this way, but an office party is still a gathering of people connected by their *jobs*. This is not a time for eating or drinking *too much*. Have fun, but always be professional!

YOUR TURN!

It's freezing!!! Are you going to a friend's for a Hanukkah celebration? Planning to spend the day in Chinatown for the Lunar New Year festivities? Trust us—you'll get cold! Dress in *layers* and bundle up!

Here are some things you'll need to stay warm—can you *match up* to *bundle up*? Answers are on page 174.

a. scarf	e. snow pants	h. ear muffs	l. ski mask
b. mittens	f. ear warmer	i. snowsuit	m. fleece
c. gloves	g. T-shirt and	j. jacket	n. down
d. beanie	flip-flops	k. coat	o. wool

1. _____ a warm material on a headband that doesn't cover the whole head; has a large, round section of warm material to cover the ears

2. _____ a really warm **synthetic** material; also what we call the sweaterlike thing that's made of that material. You can wear it under your coat.

3. _____ one piece that zips to cover top and bottom; often worn by little kids

4. _____ a short covering to go on top of all the other warm clothes

5. _____ hat made of a knit material that pulls down over the ears, and covers the whole face. There are holes for the eyes and mouth.

6. _____ material made from the curly outside of sheep!

7. _____ a cute hat made of a knit material that pulls down over the ears; sometimes has a cute ball of fabric on top

8. _____ long, narrow material of knit fabric to wrap around your neck. And face!

9. _____ the **fluffy** soft feathers of geese or ducks; used in jackets, coats, and cozy blankets

10. _____ warmers for your hands; there is a shape for each finger

11. _____ an uncovered band that goes over the head with only two fluffy round sections for the ears

12. _____ thick, **waterproof** piece to go on as a layer over pants

13. _____ Haha! Is this what our California friends wear in winter?!

14. _____ a long covering to go on top of all the other warm clothes

15. _____ warmers for your hands; there is a shape for the thumb, but the other fingers are together in one section

FUN WITH IDIOMATIC EXPRESSIONS: Light

- **burn the candle at both ends:** work and play hard, doing many things with little sleep
  *He was **burning the candle at both ends**. It sure is hard to work full time, go to school, and party at night!*

- **can't hold a candle to something/someone:** not be as good as someone/something else
  *Andy was a good student, but he **couldn't hold a candle** to his sister, who was a straight A student and star athlete.*

- **the light of one's life:** the most important person in someone's life
  *His child is **the light of his life**.*

- **shed light on something:** make something clear
  *Well, that beach postcard **sheds light on** the reason he hasn't answered his work e-mail. He's on vacation!*

- **see the light:** finally understand the importance of something
  *After refusing to wear a coat for weeks, he finally **saw the light** when the first snowfall came.*

JUST FOR FUN!

 If you can't go to a Lunar New Year festival, go to a Chinese restaurant for dinner! Americans are familiar with fortune cookies—sweet, crisp, folded cookies with a little paper inside that are served for dessert. The little papers have fun sayings or good advice written on them. Some have lucky numbers.

Go sledding! You have some days off for the holidays, yay! Okay, are you dressed for the weather? Perfect! Then go have fun! Most neighborhoods have a favorite hill for kids to slide down after it snows. But you'll need some **equipment**!

- **toboggan:** This is a long, flat wooden thing made of very smooth boards. The front curves up.
- **sled:** Like a toboggan, but it has metal strips on the bottom of each side. It's flat and doesn't curve.
- **snowboard:** Made for those crazy adventure-lovers! It's a board that you stand on to go down a snowy hill.
- **saucer:** This is a round plastic disk that you sit on. Some kids even use a trash can cover!
- **snowtube:** A round plastic inflatable thing shaped like a donut (Do NOT eat the snowtube!). You sit in the middle of the tube.
- **snowmobile:** Okay, this one is NOT for kids on a sledding hill! It's a motor vehicle that people use to travel on paths in the woods. Think of it as a little car on skis . . . fun, but be careful!

VOCABULARY

- ⓘ **ahem:** a sound made as a funny way to get someone's attention
- **coins:** change; round, metal pieces of money
- **covered:** dealt with; talked about
- **crafts:** things people make
- **craftspeople:** people who make things with special care
- **dreidel:** a special toy kids play with during Hanukkah

- **dumpling:** dough, usually around a meat or other filling, that is fried or boiled. Oh, yum . . . just thinking about it makes us hungry!
- **equipment:** things you need to do something
- **firecrackers:** small fireworks that go *CRACKcrackcrack*!
- **fluffy:** soft and light
- **gelt:** money; gold
- ⓘ **get the hang of:** become comfortable doing something after practice
- **harvest:** pick crops; also, things grown on a farm; crops; the time to pick those crops
- **in person:** face to face
- **joyous:** very, very happy
- **lanterns:** lights that can be carried
- **latkes:** yummy potato pancakes
- **loud:** TOO MUCH VOLUME!
- **menorah:** a special candle holder that keeps the candles of Hanukkah
- **parade:** musical bands, dancers and happy people marching down main streets to celebrate
- **population:** groups of people
- **principle:** a belief about how people should behave or live
- **rich:** wealthy; having lots of money
- **spin:** cause to turn in a very fast way
- **synthetic:** not made of natural materials (like plastic or man-made fabrics)
- ⓘ **top to bottom:** completely! very thoroughly
- **vendor:** a seller
- **waterproof:** won't let water in
- **wealth:** lots of money that someone has
- **wrapped:** covered

VALENTINE'S DAY

Okay, snow and ice aren't the only things in the air in February. How about something a little *warmer*? Ah yes, we're talking about . . . **L-O-V-E**! Come on, you know what holiday we're talking about now . . . Can't you tell by everyone wearing pink or red? It's Valentine's Day! It's the day of . . . *say it with us* . . . the day of . . . LOVE!

Well, we **have a confession to make**. Valentine's Day is one of those holidays we just love to hate. Bah, humbug! Are you wondering why we *don't* love the Day of Love?? Because it's kind of **goofy**! All those heart shapes . . . all those flowers . . . all those chocolates . . . Oh wait. We forgot about all those chocolates. Hmm, maybe we DO love Valentine's Day after all, ha!

Ping!!! What was that? Someone's been hit by Cupid's arrow. Yes, you'll see this mythical god of love flying all over the place on Valentine's Day. The story says that if he hits you with an arrow, you'll fall in love very soon.

The thing we don't like about Valentine's Day is the *pressure*! The *stress*! Here's why: We're lucky to have people whom we love. We're lucky to have people who love us. And one of the things that we love about each other is that we show our love *all the time*. . . in little ways: by helping each other. Or by making each other feel better when we're sad. Or by saying, "I love you." But then along comes Valentine's Day, and now **the heat is on**! We must buy the perfect card! Don't forget to buy chocolates! Oh boy, I hope there are some pretty flowers that I can afford! Oh no, I guess I have to buy some heart **jewelry**! *Aaackkkk!!!*

Do you see what we mean? The pressure! The stress! We like the *Every Day is Valentine's Day* plan better! With the *Every Day* plan, you just tell the person you love, "I love you" any time, any day. Okay, maybe that's just us. But if you want to be like most Americans, you'll give something special to your very special someone—your Valentine—on Valentine's Day, February 14. Just take a look at the supermarket on February 13 and 14. You see all those guys **snapping up** the red heart-shaped boxes of fancy chocolates? All the **bouquets** of red roses? Those guys are feeling the pressure! They don't want to be the guys who hear, "WHAT? You didn't get me anything for Valentine's Day?!"

Remember count and non-count nouns? *Chocolate* is a tricky one. It can be both.

When we're talking about our favorite treat in *general*, we say *chocolate* (non-count). When we're talking about a box of all the yummy little things, we say *chocolates*. You can count every sweet, creamy, delicious one!

And you don't need a Valentine to get a beautiful, heart-shaped box of *chocolates*; you can just buy your own. Here's a cool hint: On the day after Valentine's Day, all the fancy *chocolates* in your town will be *half-price*!

Woo hoo—*chocolate* AND a **bargain**! But if you just can't wait, buy a bar of *chocolate* . . . break off a big piece and . . . YUM! (Oh well . . . there goes that New Year's resolution.)

◀ **Now listen to Audio Track 6**
(transcript on page 203)

Okay, we admit it—we do love the little cards the kids make. (Little kids just *love* hearts, have you noticed?) In schools, making valentines and writing little notes is a traditional activity. *WATCH OUT* for the glitter! Children like to exchange valentines with their classmates, and if they do, teachers make sure that every child is included. Making sure *every* child feels loved on Valentine's Day (and *EVERY DAY*!) is a celebration we can agree with!

TAKE A LOOK: Inclusive Language

At one time in the U.S., it was very unusual to see women in some jobs. For example, in the 1950s, there were very few women firefighters. Today, however, women work in every profession. As a result, we've come to use more **inclusive** words to describe workers—words that include women.

YOUR TURN!

Take a look at the following words. Can you think of words that are more inclusive? Check our suggestions on page 175.

1. _____ actor/actress
He's a serious *actor*, but she's a funny *actress*.

2. _____ businessman
A *businessman* has lots of meetings.

3. _____ chairman

The *chairman* started the meeting by asking for coffee!

4. _____ congressman

The people voted for a *congressman* to represent them in Washington, D.C.

5. _____ fireman

Besides keeping people safe, a *fireman* helps the community.

6. _____ newsman

It's important for a *newsman* to be honest.

7. _____ man-made

Did you know this lake is *man-made*?

8. _____ freshman

A *freshman* has to learn about the school rules.

9. _____ mailman

No, little pooch! Don't bark when the *mailman* brings our mail!

10. _____ host/hostess

The *hostess* welcomed us to the restaurant.

11. _____ spokesman

The president's *spokesman* announced the new policy.

12. _____ policeman

Protecting people is a *policeman's* job.

13. _____ salesman

Great *salesman*—I bought ten new sweaters!

14. _____ waiter/waitress

Our *waitress* brought an extra dessert. Yum!

15. _____ weatherman

After a week of snow, no one liked the *weatherman*!

☑ VALENTINE'S DAY INFO TO KNOW:

We hate to tell you this, but here's what you *have* to do: Give a valentine to your **sweetie**. But we're big fans of doing it your own way: You don't have to *buy* a card . . . you can make one. In our opinion, a personal note **from the heart** is better than any supermarket card! (Just watch out for the glitter, haha!)

On Valentine's Day don't forget the people you love who may not have anyone else to be their Valentine . . . like Granny or dear old Aunt Lulu. A card or note from you can warm their *hearts* . . . and yours! Extra credit if you send them flowers, too!

 We LOVE those big boxes of fancy chocolates!

No, wait. We don't like the chocolates with coconut inside . . . Oh, and we don't like the **marshmallow** ones . . . Um . . . and we *really* don't like the ones with peanuts . . . But, hey, we LOVE the **caramels**! Ooh, and the raspberry and orange creams!

Here's a little trick we learned from Erin and James to get *only* the pieces we love:

1. Take a chocolate from the box.

2. Make sure no one is watching you.

3. With your finger, push in the *bottom* of the chocolate.

4. If it's not a piece you like, repeat step 2 and put the chocolate back in the box.

5. Try another one. HAHA!

YOUR TURN!

Here's everything you need to know about Valentine's Day! Fill in the boxes on the next page with the words or phrases that fit the categories. Answers are on page 176.

go to a restaurant

love letter

flowers

jewelry

cook a nice meal

have a **couples' spa day**

mwah! (big **smooch**)

143

surprised

excited

box of chocolates

love

a crush on someone

I love you.

Valentine (card)

a broken heart

spend a weekend in the country

I **luv** u

1432

visit someone who doesn't have a Valentine

watch a **romantic** movie at home

Things to Say, Write, or Text:

Things You Feel:

Things to Give:

Things to Do:

Chocolates? Bah, humbug! Candy hearts are another typical Valentine's Day treat. We're not sure anyone actually eats these small, hard sweet hearts—but the messages sure are fun. They say things like:

Be Mine	True Love	Hugs (OOO)
Cutie Pie	Sweetie	Kisses (XXX)
Luv	U + Me	4 ever

FUN WITH IDIOMATIC EXPRESSIONS: Hearts

We really love you! Here are a **bunch of** heart idioms—it's our Valentine to you!

- **have a change of heart:** change your mind
  *She planned to break up with him, but **had a change of heart** when she read the loving note on his Valentine card.*

- **have a heart of gold/have a big heart:** be very kind and generous
  *He has a **heart of gold**—he checks in on his elderly neighbor every day and often brings her treats.*
  *She **has a big heart**—she rescues stray animals and helps find them a good home.*

- **have your heart set on something:** to really, really, REALLY want something
  *Ten-year-old Charlotte **had her heart set on** getting the fanciest new cell phone. Sorry Charlotte. Mom says you'll have to wait a few years!*

- **be brokenhearted:** feel very, very sad when someone has died or when a love relationship ends
  *When she asked for a divorce after three years, her husband was **brokenhearted**.*

- **not have the heart to do something:** not want to do something that might make someone feel upset
  *She **didn't have the heart** to tell her son that his favorite teacher was moving away.*

- **know something by heart:** know something perfectly
  *The little kid was only three years old, but she **knew** the cartoon song **by heart**!*

- **get to the heart of something:** know what is most important about something
  *We need to **get to the heart of the problem** before we can think of a solution.*

- **eat your heart out!:** be very jealous! (This is usually said in a fun way, to tease a friend.)
  *Ha! I just got a fancy new car! **Eat your heart out**!*

- **cross my heart:** promise that something is true
  *I'll take you to Paris next year, **cross my heart**!*

- **warmhearted:** loving and kind (this is good)
  *She's so **warmhearted**—she offered to work extra hours so her friend could meet his family at the airport.*

- **coldhearted:** uncaring and mean (this is bad)
  *Her friend hadn't seen his family in two years, but his **coldhearted** boss wouldn't give him the day off to meet his family at the airport.*

- **have a heart!:** a way to ask someone to be kind to you
  *The teacher gave the kids lots of homework over the holiday. "Please, Ms. Grumpp . . . **have a heart**!" they said.*

- **take it to heart:** think about something in a very serious way
  *I gave him some advice about studying harder, and I see that he **took it to heart**. His grades are much better.*

- **from the bottom of my heart:** very sincerely; with real meaning
  *He gave her flowers and said, "I'm sorry from the **bottom of my heart** that I forgot your birthday."*

JUST FOR FUN!

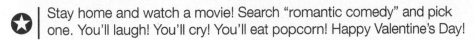

Lots of people like to go to a fancy restaurant for dinner on Valentine's Day. This may seem like a great idea . . . but . . . remember that a million other people have the same idea! Because they're so busy on this day, most restaurants offer a "special menu" with just a few choices. Service can be *v-e-r-y   s-l-o-w*, and because the chefs are so busy in the kitchen, the food may not be as fabulous as you had hoped. In our opinion—skip the restaurant dinner! Save it for a less busy time. We say, "Hello, Mr. Pizza Delivery Guy!"

Stay home and watch a movie! Search "romantic comedy" and pick one. You'll laugh! You'll cry! You'll eat popcorn! Happy Valentine's Day!

Stay at a **Bed and Breakfast** for the weekend. (You'll have to make a **reservation** MONTHS **in advance**.) It's romantic—the **scenery** is beautiful, the **inn** is pretty, the breakfast is fancy, and there's **NOTHING TO DO** . . . so you have to talk to each other! Haha!

VOCABULARY

- ⓘ **1432:** I love you too (too = 2)
- ⓘ **143:** I love you (l = **1** letter; love = **4** letters; you = **3** letters)
- • **a crush on someone:** a feeling of romantic love; feeling that you are in love with someone you don't know well
- • **bargain:** a great price for something
- • **Bed and Breakfast:** a small comfortable place to stay; provides only a room and morning breakfast
- • **bouquet:** a bunch of flowers in a group you can hold (or put in a vase)
- • **bunch of:** lots of; many
- • **caramel:** sweet, chewy candy made from butter and sugar. Ooh, I want some!
- • **couples' spa day:** a day of relaxing; enjoying massages, soaks, and spa services together
- • **from the heart:** sincerely
- ⓘ **goofy:** silly, a little funny; not serious
- • **have a confession to make:** admit something that may not be popular
- • **in advance:** before the time
- • **inclusive:** making everyone in a group feel accepted
- • **inn:** a small, comfortable hotel in the country
- • **jewelry:** metal chains and gems for decorating people!
- ⓘ **luv:** love
- • **marshmallow:** a very soft, puffy candy of creamy sugar. It's like a little cloud of sweetness!
- ⓘ **mwah!:** the sound of a really big kiss!
- • **nothing to do:** no exciting activities available
- • **pressure:** feeling forced to do something
- • **reservation:** a saved room in a hotel, or table in a restaurant
- • **romantic:** having to do with love and feelings of love
- • **scenery:** the natural beauty of an area
- ⓘ **smooch:** a big kiss
- ⓘ **snapping up:** buying very quickly before something is gone
- • **stress:** an uncomfortable feeling of emotional pressure to do something, or anxiety about doing things
- ⓘ **sweetie:** a loved one!
- ⓘ **the heat is on:** there's pressure to do this!

Answers start on page 177.

CULTURE

Decide if the best response to these statements is *yes* or *no*. If it's *no*, make the statement correct.

1. Jane and Sheila always keep their New Year's resolutions. _____

2. Abraham Lincoln was the first U.S. president. _____

3. Kwanzaa celebrates Native American culture. _____

4. Christmas Day is December 26. _____

5. Hanukkah is celebrated over six days. _____

6. Chinese New Year is celebrated on the same day every year. _____

7. If the groundhog sees his shadow, spring will come early. _____

8. Valentine's Day is a celebration of love and friendship. _____

9. Christmas Eve is the day after Christmas Day. _____

10. Schools are closed on Martin Luther King Day. _____

VOCABULARY

Complete the sentences below with a word from the following list.

hot chocolate	gloves	snowman	fire
snowdrift	slush	sled	
blizzard	snowplows	snowsuit	

Mom: Wow, did you hear the wind last night? It was blowing like crazy! And all that snow! The weather people were right with their prediction of a (11)_____.

Kid: WOO HOO! SNOW DAY!

Mom: Yeah, it sure is a snow day. We can't even open the door! The wind blew the snow into a deep (12)_____ right up against the house. We're snowed in!

Kid: WOO HOO! SNOW DAY!

Mom: The (13)_____ will be working all day to clear the roads. I'm sure we'll be able to go out tomorrow. And, lucky you, I'm sure school will be open again!

Kid: BOO!!! NO!!!

Mom: HA! YES! So why don't you go outside and enjoy it while you can. But, um, you'll have to shovel your way out the door.

Kid: Very funny, Mom. That's just a Mom way to get me to do the snow shoveling! But yeah, all the kids are texting . . . Everyone wants to go sledding, and build a giant (14)_____! Okay, I'll start shoveling and then head to the park. See you later, Mom!

Mom: WHAT?!! You can't go out like that! You'll freeze! Go put on a (15)_____.

(. . . A few minutes later . . .)

Kid: Hoo boy. Okay, is this better?

Mom: WHAT?! You can't go out like that! Your hands will freeze! Where are your (16)_____?!

Kid: They're in my pockets. Relax, Mom. I'll put them on when I get to the sledding hill. Um, but, hey, where's the (17)_____?

Mom: Hmm. I have no idea where we put it after last winter. You could just use a trash can cover, but take a look outside. If the sun keeps shining as brightly as it is now . . .

Kid: Noooo!!! Ickk! That bright sun will melt the snow on the sledding hill into (18)_____. No sledding in that stuff . . .

Mom: Well, Dad's brought in some wood . . . Why don't you just stay nice and warm inside and we'll have some family time playing games by the (19)_____

Kid: Hmm. Well, if I do that would you make me a nice mug of (20)_____? With a candy cane to stir it?

Mom: YES!!!

IDIOMATIC EXPRESSIONS

Match the idiom with its meaning.

a. work and play hard, doing many things with little sleep

b. overworked; having a TON of things to do

c. stop the uncomfortable feeling people have with a new group; do something to make strangers begin talking

d. the most important person in someone's life

e. loving and kind

f. finally understand the importance of something

g. not want to do something that might make someone feel upset

h. really, really, REALLY want something

i. change your mind

j. become nervous about something you had planned to do, and change your mind

21. _____ see the light
22. _____ the light of one's life
23. _____ warmhearted
24. _____ get cold feet
25. _____ have your heart set on something
26. _____ burn the candle at both ends
27. _____ break the ice
28. _____ have a change of heart
29. _____ snowed under
30. _____ not have the heart to do something

SPRING

SPRING

SPRUCE UP—IT'S SPRING!

Aaah . . . aaah . . . *aaahCHOO!* That can mean only one thing: It's spring! Flowers and new leaves and growing grass and . . . **pollen**! Yes, springtime is also **allergy** season—when many people have a **reaction** to pollen in the air. Hey! Where are the **tissues**?! Ha, maybe we used them all when our winter colds and flu made us **sneeze**! The change of seasons can be **dicey**. Did that groundhog **predict** six more weeks of winter? And how about the traditional farmers' saying, "If March comes in like a lion, it goes out like a lamb"? (That predicts that if the beginning of March is cold and **harsh**, then the end of the month will be mild and nice.) Predictions, predictions! Why can't someone predict a **cure** for allergies?

IDES OF MARCH

Groundhogs and farmers predicting the weather! That reminds us of another famous prediction—

Do you remember learning about the **ancient history** of Rome? How about reading Shakespeare? Does the **warning**, "**Beware** the Ides of March" **ring a bell**? Extra points for you! That prediction said the middle of March (March 15, *the Ides*) would be very unlucky for Julius Caesar. It was! He was killed on March 15 in 44 B.C.

Well, whether from colds or spring allergies, all that sneezing is no fun, but we sure love the happier signs of spring:

The birds are **chirping**; the flowers are **blooming**; the grass is growing;

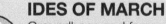

and people are finally getting out of the house after a long, cold, dark winter. These are the days we've been waiting for!

And the days are about to get longer. **Daylight Saving Time** means one more hour of sunlight (yay!), but setting the clock ahead on the second Sunday in March means lots of **yawns** at the office the following workday. The alarm clock may say, "It's 7:00," but your poor, tired body is saying, "Wait a minute! It's only 6:00! Go back to sleep!" But you can't go back to sleep! There's work to be done! Your weekends will be busy, busy, busy with yard work—pulling **weeds**, **trimming** trees, and planting flowers and **veggies**. All that nice green grass that's growing? That beautiful **lawn** you've been waiting for all winter? Somebody better get out there and **mow** it! Oh boy. Let's hope the **lawnmower** still works!

Sure, everyone loves to be outside in the nice spring weather . . . unless it's **raining cats and dogs**. We have a saying in English: "April showers bring May flowers." Yes, the weather is getting nice, but we're happy to have *some* rain, too.

RAIN RAIN GO AWAY

Don't be **shy**—sing it with us: *"Rain, rain, go away. Come again another day!"*

We have lots of words for rain! Each one has a slightly different meaning. (We think it's because the weather announcers just get bored. Ha!) Here are some:

- **drizzle:** a very light, continuous rain
- **shower:** a short period of light rain
- **downpour:** a heavy rain that starts suddenly
- **hail:** tiny frozen drops or golf-ball sized pieces of ice. Yes, *ice!* LOOK OUT!
- **"It's pouring!"** and **"It's coming down in buckets!":** both mean it's raining very heavily. (And some people say, "It's raining hard.")

◀ **Now listen to Audio Track 7**
(transcript on page 205)

Those spring rain showers give us a perfect chance to get started inside with spring cleaning. You may know the custom of cleaning the house **from top to bottom** as a New Year tradition in many countries. With the nice spring weather finally here, people in the U.S. like to open the windows and **freshen** and clean *everything*. Okay, maybe we should say *most* people like to clean everything, ha! (We'd rather read a book. Or feed the cat. Or find **loose change** in the sofa cushions. Or . . . well, you get the idea.)

Spring brings a special holiday, too. These sunny, warm (cleaning!) days are the perfect time to think of Mom. (No, no, no! *Not* because of the *cleaning* . . . because of the sunny, warm, HAPPY part!) Americans celebrate their moms on Mother's Day—always the second Sunday in May. Little kids work with Dad to make breakfast, and then they bring those blueberry chocolate chip banana fudge pancakes(!) to Mom on a **tray**, with a flower and handmade **cards**. Breakfast in bed—a special treat! Well, Mom may not think the food is such a special treat (after all, Dad's not much of a cook in our house, ha!), but she sure loves the little cards that the kids make. In fact, most moms' refrigerators are like little art galleries for their kids' art and creations! Older kids and adults give their moms cards, flowers, chocolates, and presents, or they may all go out for a special restaurant dinner. We love you, Mom!

MOM

We love Mom! We're pretty sure everyone everywhere thinks moms are super. Did you ever wonder why the word *mom* is sometimes capitalized, and sometimes not? Easy! When we use a family title in place of the person's name, we capitalize it. When you were a kid, weren't you surprised to learn that your mom had another name besides the only name you knew: *Mom?*

Hey, Dad, when you finish the spring cleaning, can we take Mom out to lunch? We know that moms everywhere love special treats. Okay, dads like special treats too, right, Dad? Hey, let's invite Grandma because grandmas deserve a special treat, too!

Yes, the spring season has lots of happy holidays to go along with the great weather. Hmm, well, the weather's great when it's not raining, anyway. **Spring fever** is everywhere! Come on, get off the couch and go outside! Breathe in that fresh spring air!

TAKE A LOOK: Foreign Abbreviations in English

All those predictions got us thinking. . . . Who could have predicted that so much of ancient Latin would be used in modern-day English? Here's a group of abbreviations that are very common in English. Some are academic, some are used in business, and some are from our shopping list! (N.B.—don't forget the vegetables!) See how many you notice in everyday use.

etc. (*et cetera*): and other stuff
*I need to buy party supplies: snacks, plates, cups, napkins, **etc.***

e.g. (*exampli gratia*): for example
*There are lots of things you can use to make a Mother's Day card (**e.g.**, colored paper and paper plates).*

i.e. (*id est*): in other words
*He spends most of his time social networking, online shopping, and Web surfing, **i.e.**, on the computer.*

C.V. (*curriculum vitae*): a kind of short résumé
*The first thing the employer asked for was a copy of his **C.V.***

IV (*intravenous*): within the vein
*I know hospital patients get **IV** medicine, but there are days at work when I wish I could have an IV of coffee!*

A.D. (*anno Domini*): in the year of the Lord, time measured from the birth of Christ
*The Mayan city of Chichen Itza was still important in **A.D.** 900.*

B.C. (Before Christ): time measured from before the birth of Christ
*Some Egyptian pyramids were built around 2000 **B.C.***

C.E. (Common Era): the A.D. years without using the Christian reference
*In modern usage, **C.E.** refers to the A.D. years.*

B.C.E. (Before Common Era): the B.C. years without using the Christian reference
*In modern usage, **B.C.E.** refers to the B.C. years.*

P.S. (*post-scriptum*): A thought after writing!
*Her letter described a wonderful vacation, but we didn't know where she was . . . until she wrote, "**P.S.** I'm in Paris!"*

RIP (*requiescat in peace*): Rest in peace
> *The singer's fans were sad to hear of his death. Social networks online were filled with messages saying, "RIP."*

vs. (versus): against
> *The New York Mets **vs.** the Philadelphia Phillies—what a game!*

N.B. (*nota bene*): Note well! Take notice! Pay attention!
> *We're planning a fun trip to Brazil in May. **N.B.**: Seasons in North America and South America are opposite, so bring the right clothes!*

YOUR TURN!

Can you fill in the blanks with the correct foreign abbreviations listed above? Answers are on page 179.

1. The Egyptian pyramids were built around 2500 _____.

2. The Huns invaded Europe around _____ 360.

3. In the battle of the lawns, it's man _____ weeds!

4. What? You're still in bed? You should be mowing the lawn and pulling weeds, _____, working in the garden!

5. _____: The meeting is canceled, but reports are still due today!

6. "Thanks for inviting us. We had a great time! _____ I almost forgot to tell you! The group will be meeting at my house next week."

7. Remember to buy special treats for Mom, like candy, cards, flowers, _____.

8. Don't forget to get some breakfast things, _____, strawberries, orange juice, and muffins.

9. I'm sad that the tree we planted last spring didn't survive the cold winter. _____, apple tree.

10. If you're looking for a new job, make sure your _____ is **up to date** with your experience.

FUN WITH IDIOMATIC EXPRESSIONS: Spring Bonus

- **spring something on someone:** surprise someone with something unexpected (usually with something that's not a good idea!)
  *I hate to **spring this on you**, but you only have ten minutes to finish all your shopping before the store closes.*

- **spring into action:** suddenly make a move to do something
  *Tony was relaxing all day watching the soccer game; when the rain clouds moved in we watched him **spring into action**. Yes, Tony, hurry! Mow the grass before it starts pouring!*

- **no spring chicken:** not young; um. . . old
  *She's **no spring chicken**, but she can still swim a mile a day!*

- **spring up:** occur suddenly
  *In New York City, it seems like a new restaurant **springs up** every week.*

- **spring for something:** pay for something to treat someone else
  *Hey, everybody, come on down to the conference room! The boss said he'll **spring for pizza**!*

VOCABULARY

- **allergy:** a reaction to spring pollen, or other things; sometimes symptoms are like having a cold
- **ancient history:** the time before the year A.D. 1 (or 1 C.E.)
- **beware:** watch out! be careful of something dangerous
- **blooming:** bursting into flower
- **cards:** 1. Folded notes with pictures and messages, often given on special occasions such as birthdays. 2. special packs of fifty-two for games or tricks
- **chirping:** the sound a happy bird makes
- **cure:** a medicine that will heal; make a sickness go away
- **Daylight Saving Time:** changing the clocks an hour to add sunlight hours to the day
- ⓘ **dicey:** uncertain; left to chance
- **freshen:** make everything smell clean
- **from top to bottom:** all over
- **harsh:** severe
- **lawn:** an area of grass, often around a house
- **lawnmower:** the machine that cuts the grass!

- **loose change:** coins
- **mow:** cut grass
- **pollen:** yellow-green dust from flowers that makes you sneeze
- **predict:** say what will happen in the future
- ⓘ **raining cats and dogs:** raining very hard. Why cats and dogs? We have absolutely no idea!
- **reaction:** way a person responds to something
- ⓘ **ring a bell:** make you remember something; sound familiar; remind you of something that you know
- **shy:** timid
- **sneeze:** aaah...aaah.....*aaahCHOO!*
- **spring fever:** term used to describe the excitement people feel in spring ("I don't want to go to work! I want to sit outside in the sunshine!")
- **tissues:** disposable paper cloths for sneezing and other cold symptoms
- **tray:** small, flat carrier for food and drinks
- **trimming:** cutting (also, especially at Christmas: decorating)
- **up to date:** having the newest information; most recent
- ⓘ **veggies:** vegetables
- **warning:** advice about something dangerous
- **weeds:** nuisance plants that grow among the flowers. Pull them out! Hey... While you're at it, come get ours!
- **yawn:** just saying it makes us want to do it! s-t-r-e-t-c-h-i-n-g the mouth to show you are tired.

ST. PATRICK'S DAY

Okay, we know what you're thinking: St. Patrick is IRISH, not American. You're right! Well, sort of . . . Although he is the **patron saint** of Ireland, most people believe that St. Patrick was not actually Irish. But celebrating his day is a perfect example of how people of different cultures have become part of American culture. On March 17 lots of Americans celebrate St. Patrick's Day (some people call it "St. Paddy's Day" for fun), and everyone wants to be Irish! Look around. Everyone's wearing green! Americans of Irish

heritage are proud to show it. People who aren't Irish **get in on the fun**, too. They may wear silly hats and T-shirts that say, "Kiss Me, I'm Irish!" The color green is everywhere. Why green? Ireland's nickname is the **Emerald Isle**. If you've ever visited, you've seen its beautiful green hills and countryside. But how did the celebration start here in the U.S.? You may know that in the nineteenth century, Ireland experienced a terrible **famine**, and so a huge **influx** of Irish immigrants came to the U.S. They brought their celebration of Ireland's patron saint with them. Today St. Patrick's Day is a celebration of Ireland and its culture, with some fun American **touches**.

RAINBOWS

Who doesn't love a rainbow? When you see one in the sunshine after it rains, don't you call your friend to the window? "Hey, come look at the rainbow! It's so beautiful. Quick—take a picture and let's post it to the Internet!"

When we were kids we learned that the rainbow has seven colors: violet, indigo, blue, green, yellow, orange, and red. Some people say that there are only six colors, because indigo is just another kind of blue. Six... seven... we don't care. We just love rainbows!

The most popular symbols of St. Paddy's Day are **leprechauns**, **shamrocks**, and **rainbows** with **pots** of **gold** (we'll take the pot of gold, thank you very much!). A leprechaun is a tiny, magical man with red hair and a beard, dressed in green (of course!). Leprechauns love to play jokes on people.

Just ask our little friend, Charlotte. She says that a leprechaun comes into her house during the night and turns over all the furniture. She tries to catch him in a **trap**, but he's too **tricky**. Hmm. Why would anyone want to catch this little guy? Well, remember all that gold! Leprechauns have tons of it that they hide in pots at the end of rainbows. If you catch the little guy, maybe *you* can trick *him* into telling you where it's hidden! (But probably not. Leprechauns are really smart and very hard to trick.) Tradition says that a leprechaun will give three wishes to a human who catches him. Good luck!

Speaking of luck, . . . shamrocks and **four-leaf clovers** are also **good luck** symbols of the holiday. To celebrate St. Paddy's Day, some people will paint their faces with a shamrock or four-leaf clover. Do you think that's crazy? We think *this* is crazy: Some cities **dye** their rivers green for the day, and lots of local **watering holes** dye the beer green! We're not kidding! And of course there are lots of parades in every big city, with **marchers** playing **bagpipes**, and students proudly showing their Irish dancing skills. Oh yes, and it's another great excuse for a party. People like to decorate cookies and cakes with green **sprinkles**, and some even dye their food and drinks green. ICK!

(When the food in *our* **fridge** turns green, we know it's time to throw it out, ha!) The traditional St. Patrick's Day foods are **corned beef** and **cabbage** with boiled potatoes and Irish **soda bread**. YUM!

 If this sounds like your kind of fun (and you really love the color green, ha!), you should plan to visit Savannah, Georgia; New York City; Boston, Massachusetts; or Chicago, Illinois. These cities have HUGE St. Patrick's Day celebrations. Make your reservations early!

TAKE A LOOK: Shades of Color

We have tons of words to describe colors. Why just say *purple* when you can say *aubergine*? Why say *brown* when you can say *café au lait*? Ha! We're not even sure what all these shades of color are. . . . Sometimes we think fashion designers just make them up! And really, did you ever wonder why so many colors are named after *food*?

 COLORS
Hey, what color is your hair? Do you think that's an easy question to answer? Ha! You may think that *brunette* (brown), *blonde* (yellow-ish), *black*, or *red* (really orange-ish!) would be enough. WRONG! If you're looking for an interesting new hair color, you have a lot of choices: chestnut brown, caramel, and mahogany; ash blonde, golden blonde, and champagne; midnight black and ebony; dark red, auburn, burgundy . . . YIKES! We don't want to eat the stuff; we just want to hide our gray hairs! (But, shhh. That's our little secret . . . ☺)

Hey, did you see what we just did? We wanted to say that a color was not true yellow, but *kind of* yellow (yellow-ish); not actual orange, but *kind of* orange (orange-ish).

Adding that little *-ish* to a word shows that we mean *kind of*, *approximately*, *not exactly*.

Here are some more examples of how you can use *-ish*:

- "Hey, what time is the party?"
- "7-ish."

- "I hear she has a really big dog."
- "Well, it's a Labrador. It's big-ish, but not really huge."

- "Nice sweater! Is it new?"
- "New-ish, I guess. I bought it last month."

◀ **Now listen to Audio Track 8**
(transcript on page 206)

YOUR TURN!

Look at the following shades of color. Can you put the color words from the list into the correct category? (Did you spot our old friend *indigo* from the rainbow?) Use your dictionary (and imagination!) to check any you don't know. DON'T EAT THE COLOR WORDS!!! Answers are on page 179.

apricot	fuchsia	scarlet	slate
blush	~~indigo~~	mint	navy
charcoal	ivory	onyx	buttercup
chocolate	jet	plum	ruby
coffee	lavender	silver	tangerine
cream	lime	mustard	olive
crimson	pearl	rose	tan
denim	ebony	lemon	salmon
			violet

Black _____

_____

White _____

_____

Gray _____

_____

Brown _____

_____

Blue _____indigo_____

_____

Red_____

_____

Orange _____

_____

Yellow _____

_____

Purple _____

_____

Pink _____

_____

Green _____

_____

 JUST FOR FUN!

 Wear something green! Everyone gets in on the fun. But do NOT try to kiss someone, even if their shirt says, "Kiss me, I'm Irish!"

 Plan a party. Decorate with lots of green: **balloons** and **garlands**, **tablecloth** and **paper goods**. Buy some treats, like cupcakes with green **frosting**, and put a drop of green **food coloring** into lemon soda. Give your guests **party favors** like small chocolate coins wrapped in gold. We'll **be right over**! If you're invited to a party, you could bring an Irish treat. "Irish potatoes" (sweet, soft candies shaped to look like tiny potatoes) are a fun idea.

 Why are potatoes sometimes associated with the Irish? Potatoes were a hugely important food crop in Ireland around the time of the famine in the mid-nineteenth century. For many people it was the main food source. When the potato crop failed for several years, many Irish people died of **starvation**. Many others came to the U.S. The potato famine was a terrible time in Irish history, but Americans are glad to enjoy the culture that the Irish brought here.

YOUR TURN!

Complete the sentences with St. Patrick's Day words. Answers are on page 180.

1. St. Patrick's Day is also called _____ for fun.

2. _____ are small green plants with three leaves; they're typical St. Patrick's Day decorations.

3. That little _____ plays lots of tricks, and the kids will never catch him!

4. If you ever find the end of a(n) _____, you may find a pot of gold. (Call us if you do!)

5. Bagpipes and Irish dancing are fun parts of the _____ on St. Patrick's Day.

6. Many Irish people came to the U.S. because of a terrible _____ in Ireland when people had no food to eat.

7. A(n) _____ is a beautiful green **gemstone** used in jewelry.

JEWELRY

Are you looking for a gift idea for someone special? Everyone loves jewelry. Um. . . including *us*. Ha! Here are some ideas for you. Or. . .us!

- **jewelry:** earrings, rings, necklaces, and bracelets. Silver and gold chains are beautiful and very popular choices for jewelry.
- **bracelet:** worn on the wrist
- **necklace:** worn around the neck
- **ring:** worn on a finger
- **earrings:** worn in or around the ears
- **gemstones:** expensive (usually colored) stones; these are often mined—dug from inside the earth. We love sparkling green emeralds!

◀ **Now listen to Audio Track 9**
(transcript on page 206)

8. Sometimes people like to give their guests a small party _____ to take home after the party.

9. A pretty _____ will protect your table from all that green food!

10. _____ is a favorite choice for dinner on St. Patrick's Day. Okay, well, it's OUR favorite choice!

FUN WITH IDIOMATIC EXPRESSIONS: Green!

You'll see plenty of green on St. Patrick's Day. There are also lots of idioms with the word *green*.

- **get the green light for something:** get official approval to start a new project
  *The developer was happy to **get the green light** to build a gambling casino in Philadelphia. The people who lived near the project were not so happy.*

- **look green around the gills:** look sick.
  *The new guy is at home sick today. He did **look a little green around the gills** yesterday.*

- **have a green thumb:** be very successful growing plants
  *Jane's garden is always beautiful; she really **has a green thumb**.*

- **go green:** do things that show care for the environment
  *I'm trying to **go green**. I recycle as much as I can, and no more water in plastic bottles!*

- **be green with envy:** be very jealous
  *Ha! when she sees my new car she'll **be green with envy**!*

✓ ST. PATRICK'S DAY INFO TO KNOW:

Good luck! Everyone wants it! Sometimes people do crazy things to get the success and happiness that we call good luck. Here are some things that are traditionally considered lucky . . . or unlucky! (Take your pick!)

Lucky

- See a rainbow (double-lucky if you see a double rainbow).
- Find a four-leaf clover (good luck trying!).
- Cross your fingers.
- Blow out all the candles on your birthday cake in one breath. (Whew. In our case, somebody better call the firefighters!)

- Make number 7 your lucky number.
- See a **ladybug**. (If you find this cute little insect, tradition says you should blow it away safely into the yard, and say, "Ladybug, ladybug, fly away home!")

 Let the kids have a contest to see who gets their lucky wish to come true. After dinner, take the **wishbone** from the chicken or turkey. Let it dry, then let the kids each take a side. Pull, kids, pull! Whoever breaks off the bigger part gets to make a wish. Good luck, kids! Make it a good wish!

Unlucky

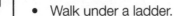

- Let a black cat cross in front of you.
- The number 13 is unlucky, and Friday the 13th is unluckiest of all! STAY HOME!
- Walk under a ladder.
- Open an umbrella inside the house.
- Break a **mirror** (you'll get seven years of bad luck! *Nooooooo!*)

 Next time you're in a hotel elevator, take a look at the buttons for each floor. Do you see the 13th floor? Many hotels (and other buildings) don't have a 13th floor. Uh-oh! Does this mean there's a big hole in the building? It's pretty funny to think about that, but no… It just means that the 14th floor is really the 13th floor! Ha! Be careful when you make your reservation!

FUN WITH IDIOMATIC EXPRESSIONS: Luck!

- **beginner's luck:** doing very well at something you have never done before, especially a sport or game
  *It was his very first time playing golf, and he got a hole-in-one! I guess it's **beginner's luck**.*
- **better luck next time:** when something goes wrong, saying this may make someone feel better
  *I'm sorry you failed your driving test yesterday. You'll have a chance to take it again, so **better luck next time**!*

- **down on one's luck:** going through a bad time when everything seems to be going wrong

*She's really **down on her luck**. First, she lost her phone, then her car died, she lost her job, and her boyfriend left her. Wow. Somebody find her a rainbow!*

- **lucky streak:** when you seem to be winning all the games you play
*I had a great time in Las Vegas! I had a **lucky streak** and won at everything.*

- **take pot luck:** take/get whatever is available
*She forgot to order tickets in advance, so when she arrived at the concert she **took pot luck** on available seats.*

POT LUCK

We use the expression *take pot luck* to mean take a chance on something. If you haven't reserved your seat on the plane, you have to *take pot luck* when you check in. You have to take a chance that a good seat will be available. Haha! Good luck with that!

Pot luck also means a certain type of informal meal. A pot luck lunch or dinner means everyone will bring something to eat and share with the others. This is a great chance to enjoy being with friends and to try lots of different delicious foods. (If you're really *lucky*, your friends, will be better cooks than we are, haha!)

VOCABULARY

- **bagpipes:** instruments made with, yes, a bag and yes, some pipes! The bag goes under your arm. It makes a very shrill sound.
- **balloons:** very colorful latex or rubber inflatables. Kids love them! Fill them with air or helium.
- ⓘ **be right over:** coming over now
- **cabbage:** large round green vegetable with lots of leaves that is most often cooked.
- **corned beef:** salted beef prepared with spices
- **dye:** (v.) give something color, or change color; (n.) the name of the stuff you use to change the color!
- **emerald:** an expensive green stone used in jewelry
- **famine:** a time when farm crops fail and there is no food

- **food coloring:** drops of liquid that change the color of your food
- **four-leaf clover:** good luck finding one of these—a small green plant hiding in the grass
- **fridge:** put your food in here to keep it cool (because no one likes to take time to pronounce *refrigerator*!)
- **frosting:** very sweet cream that goes on top of cakes and cookies; also called *icing*. . . Yum!
- **garlands:** long strings of flowers or shapes that can be used for decoration
- **gemstone:** expensive stone used in jewelry
- ① **get in on the fun:** join the fun
- **gold:** expensive yellow metal; if you're thinking of a birthday gift, this always works well!
- **good luck:** good fortune; having good things happen to you
- **heritage:** customs and culture depending on where someone's family was born
- **influx:** entry
- **isle:** island
- **ladybug:** a cute brownish-red insect with black spots
- **leprechaun:** a small magical man dressed in green, with a red beard
- **marchers:** people walking in a parade
- **mirror:** that glass you look into to see yourself. (Oh no! Is that spinach in my teeth?)
- **paper goods:** paper plates, cups, and other disposable dinnerware. (Not very environmentally friendly, but they sure save on cleanup!)
- **party favors:** small gifts people can take home to remember a party
- **patron saint:** a special saint of a country or activity (St. Christopher is the patron saint of travelers)
- **plan:** prepare; make arrangements for an event
- **pot:** large container for cooking
- **rainbow:** the curve of beautiful colors in the sky when rain mixes with sunlight
- **shamrock:** a small green plant with three leaves
- **soda bread:** No, it's not made from Coca-Cola! A traditional type of Irish bread sometimes made with raisins
- **sprinkles:** tiny colorful pieces of candy you put on cakes, cookies, and ice cream; also called *jimmies* in some places

- **starvation:** very serious hunger as a result of having no food to eat
- **tablecloth:** put this on your table to keep it clean
- **touches:** small additions
- **trap:** used to catch an animal (or a leprechaun!)
- ⓘ **tricky:** smart in making fun of people and tricking them; also very complicated
- ⓘ **watering hole:** a bar, or tavern; a place to go and have an alcoholic drink with friends (this is also the phrase for the place animals in the wild go to drink)
- **wishbone:** the bone in a chicken or turkey shaped like a U

SPRINGING INTO NICE WEATHER HOLIDAYS!

In many places spring is a time of new beginnings. Symbols of new life are everywhere, and these symbols are important in many religious celebrations. Because of the many religious groups in the U.S., there are hundreds of religious holidays celebrated throughout the year in cities across the country. Some of these religious holidays are very well known, and some are not very familiar to all. For example, Bahá'í New Year and Ridván Festivals are two traditional holidays celebrated in spring by some Americans. But some of the religious celebrations are more familiar because of their **secular observance**. For example, you're probably familiar with Carnival, but you may not know it's to mark a religious time (the beginning of Christian **Lent**). In the U.S. we celebrate Carnival as **Mardi Gras** (yes, we use the French words for "fat Tuesday" and, let's face it, the French sounds MUCH better!).

The most famous Mardi Gras party is in New Orleans, Louisiana. It's a crazy street party, with people wearing colorful **costumes** and **masks**. The streets are decorated, and big crowds watch the parades. **Partygoers** on **elaborate floats** throw **beads**, **fake** coins, and other small gifts to the **onlookers**. It's a wild time, with lots of good food and partying, before the Christian time of Lent and **sacrifice** begins.

Some people eat a special **pastry** called King Cake. Baked inside the cake is a tiny plastic toy shaped like a baby. The person who gets the piece of cake with the baby inside . . . think it's *lucky*? Haha! The tradition says that person must have the next big party! Start planning! Start shopping for party snacks! Oh yeah, and be careful not to break a tooth or **choke** on the toy baby. That would *really* be unlucky!

After the days of Lent comes Easter, when Christians celebrate the **resurrection** of Christ. It's a very important religious holiday but also a time when everyone thinks about the new life that spring brings. **Chicks** and eggs are symbols of this season of new life. In fact, a fun traditional activity is to dye Easter eggs. (Fun—except for the people who have to clean up the colorful mess later! We're looking at *you*, Mom!) Try it: Just boil some eggs and dye them with the kids. Make sure they're hard-boiled (the eggs, not the kids. Haha!). Even adults **look forward to** making the beautiful designs that they see in magazines. And, of course, many children look forward to a visit from the **Easter Bunny**. We love that big crazy bunny! In our house he leaves a **trail** of **jelly beans** leading to a **yummy** Easter basket filled with chocolate eggs, a chocolate bunny, more jelly beans, and some marshmallow chicks.

And here's something funny: Everyone has a favorite way to eat a chocolate bunny! Some people like to break off small pieces at a time. Our favorite way? Bite off those big bunny ears! Yum! But that's not all the Easter Bunny does. He also hides the dyed eggs and colored plastic eggs filled with treats. On Easter morning, the kids search for the hidden eggs. I guess you could say it's eggs-citing! (**Get it?**) You can probably also guess that all those hard-boiled eggs mean lots of egg salad sandwiches for lunch . . . for a *month*! Eggs-actly!

Another religious holiday that happens in spring is the Jewish holiday of Passover. Based on the lunar calendar, Passover commemorates an important time in Jewish history, and it's celebrated by a special dinner called a **seder**. It's a tradition to tell the story of the holiday at the dinner, and a special seder **plate** is prepared. Each food on the plate has a special meaning. Passover is a time for remembering, and for family gatherings and traditional foods.

Of course, many holiday times are set by the **lunar** calendar. This means that dates may change from year to year. One of these holidays that is very important to Muslims is Ramadan. This is a month of prayer, and **fasting** each day until the sun goes down. It's a time when many people help charities. At the end of the month, the Eid al-Fitr—a time of **feasting**, family, and giving money to the **poor**—is celebrated.

Many Americans—many religions! But one of the important aspects of American government is "separation of church and state." This means that the government does not support any one religion. Public places like schools and libraries celebrate only secular holidays. Although popular religious events occur in March or April, most universities and public schools don't celebrate them. Most schools do have a secular spring break—a holiday that lasts for a week or two when the schools are closed. Students enjoy this time off before they begin the countdown to summer vacation. During spring break older kids sometimes go away in large groups to a resort area. Trust us. You do NOT want to be in the same resort area as kids on spring break, ha!

TAKE A LOOK: Foreign Expressions You Need to Know!

"VENI, VIDI, VICI!"
Do you know those famous words by Julius Caesar? He was feeling pretty good about himself after winning a battle, and he said, "I came, I saw, I **conquered**!" Come on, admit it. Don't you sometimes feel that way when you figure out something tricky in English? Of course, there's always another battle—and in English that can sometimes be understanding how non-English words and expressions have been **adopted** into English.

Let's take a look at some common foreign expressions, how they are pronounced, their meanings, and how the words would be used in a sentence.

paparazzi: /*papa-**rot**-see*/—annoying celebrity photographers
  *The **paparazzi** waited in tents outside the movie star's apartment. As soon as she walked outside, the cameras started flashing.*

carpe diem: /*car-pay **dee**-um*/— Seize the day! Take advantage of today's opportunities. (In text-speak: **YOLO**, **Y**ou **O**nly **L**ive **O**nce.)
  *His friends were nervous about hiking the dangerous path, but he said, "**Carpe diem!**" and began the climb. After all, YOLO.*

mea culpa: /*may-uh **cull**-puh*/— my fault, my mistake
  *The magazine admitted that it didn't check the information before printing the story, so the editor wrote a **mea culpa** for the next issue.*

caveat: /**kah**-vay-ot/—a warning
*Sure, you can borrow my phone, but a **caveat**: The battery needs to be charged soon.*

non sequitur: /non **seck**-wi-tor/—a conclusion that doesn't make sense with what came before (sometimes used to change the subject from something uncomfortable)
*The car dealer said, "This car was driven by a little old lady, and she kept it in the garage." But when the customer asked if the engine needed work, the dealer said, "It's a nice, clean car!" The customer knew that **non sequitur** meant bad news about the engine.*

quid pro quo: /kwid pro kwo/—giving something to get something else
*Politicians are a tricky bunch! There's always a **quid pro quo** when they talk about passing a bill. "Okay, I'll vote for your bill if you add some benefit for my state."*

bon voyage: /bone voy-**ahj**/— Have a great trip!
*So you leave tomorrow on your Caribbean cruise! **Bon voyage**!*

résumé: /**rez**-oom-ay/— summary of job experience
*Before he applied for a new position in his company, he prepared a **résumé** to show his experience as a manager.*

graffiti: /gruh-**fee**-tee/— painting or drawing on property
*New York City cleaned the **graffiti** from all its subway cars, but the tourists missed seeing the crazy art.*

Banksy is a mysterious street artist whose graffiti on walls and bridges is considered to be modern art. People aren't sure who *he* is, but his graffiti is famous!

Keith Haring (who died in 1990) began as a New York City graffiti artist. His art now hangs in important museums all over the world.

ad lib: /ad lib/— speak without prepared words
*The comedian had to **ad lib** when the TV host unexpectedly asked him to perform.*

carte blanche: /kart blonsh/—freedom to do something any way you want
*Because Erin had traveled all over the world, her friends gave her **carte blanche** to plan their group vacation.*

feng shui: /*fung shway*/—Chinese way of arranging objects to create harmony and flow of energy

> *Yu-Ching helped her friend use* **feng shui** *to arrange furniture and plants in the new house to bring positive energy.*

ciao: /*chow*/; **adios** /*a-dee-os*/; **ta ta** /*ta-ta*/— good-bye (Note: These expressions are used very casually, among friends.)

> *Hey, I'm late for a meeting.* **Ciao***!*

alumni: (men) /*a-lum-nye*/; **alumnae** (women) /*a-lum-knee*/— graduates of a school (Note: Sometimes people use an informal short form: *alum* (singular) or *alums* (plural) for these words.)

> *The* **alumni** *decided to have a ten-year reunion. And they decided to include the* **alumnae** *of the university in the next town.*

YOUR TURN!

Using the expressions from the foreign expressions list, identify which foreign expression is described. Answers are on page 180.

1. Sure, I'll let you use my car if I can borrow your emerald necklace! _____

2. He painted a design on the wall of the building. Is it art or a criminal act? _____

3. Oh boy. I know I'm really late. Sorry! _____

4. What? You don't know the words to the song? Okay, just sing whatever comes to mind! _____

5. Do you think it's an invasion of privacy when these people follow celebrities to sell pictures to magazines? _____

6. After four days home in bed with the flu, she decided to go out and do something exciting! _____

7. Oh, you'd like to know my opinion of your singing voice? Um, wow, it's a beautiful day! _____

8. Wow, your apartment looks beautiful! I'll give you _____ if you'll come decorate mine.

9. The association collected money to create a student scholarship for its old school. _____

10. I enjoyed having coffee with you, but now I have to get back to work. _____

11. The architect planned the building with attention to how good energy would flow through the entrances. _____

12. Yes, I recommend the Washington, D.C., metro system, with one _____: the trains do not run twenty-four hours a day.

13. Hey, have a fabulous time on your vacation! _____

14. With every new job she took, she learned new skills to add to the list of her job experience. _____

☑ NICE WEATHER HOLIDAY INFO TO KNOW:

☑ Many neighborhoods have **egg hunts** for all the neighborhood kids. You can **donate** some plastic eggs filled with candy. Make sure the candy is wrapped, and avoid chocolate. (Remember that those eggs may be outside in the sun for a while. I don't think we need to tell you that chocolate + sun = icky sticky mess!)

YOUR TURN!

Part of the fun of Mardi Gras is dressing up and putting on makeup. Can you put these words into the right place in the story? Answers are on page 181.

costume	perfume	toothbrush
toothpaste	shampoo	blush
hair dryer	lipstick	eyebrow pencil
mascara	conditioner	nail polish

Maria was really excited as she got ready for the Mardi Gras celebration. First, she washed her hair with (1) _____ and then used (2) _____ to make it soft. She dried and styled it with a (3) _____. Perfect! Her hair was ready to go. Next she brushed her teeth to get that nice, minty fresh breath. She squeezed some (4) _____ onto her (5) _____. Much better! Then she put on her makeup.

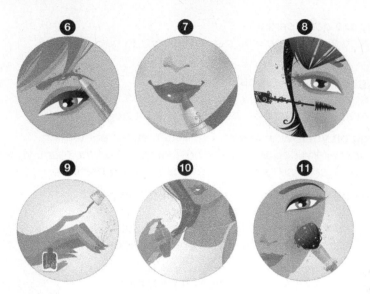

Write the words (from the list) for each picture:

(6) _____

(7) _____

(8) _____

(9) _____

(10) _____

(11) _____

Hair? Perfect! Makeup? Perfect! Now all she had to do was put on her mask and (12)_____, and she was ready to go! Have fun, Maria!

FUN WITH IDIOMATIC EXPRESSIONS: Eggs!

Have you tried to order eggs for breakfast in an American restaurant? It can be very complicated. How do you want your eggs cooked? **Scrambled, poached, boiled**? Soft-boiled or hard-boiled? Do you want them fried **over easy** or **sunny side up**? How about an **omelet**? Haha, maybe you'd rather just skip the eggs and have toast!

◀ **Now listen to Audio Track 10**
(transcript on page 207)

- **good egg:** a good person
  *She is such a **good egg**; she's always happy to help with any project.*

- **bad egg:** a bad person/troublemaker
  *Her mom was nervous about the new boyfriend. She said, "I wish you weren't dating that boy; he looks like a **bad egg** to me."*

- **have egg on your face:** feel embarrassed about something
  *Joanna told everyone she was the best swimmer on the team. When she finished last in the race, she really had **egg on her face**.*

- **walk on eggshells:** be very careful what you say and do so someone doesn't become upset
  *I think the new supervisor makes people nervous. She gets angry very easily, so people feel like they have to **walk on eggshells** around her.*

- **nest egg:** money savings put away for the future
  *It's important to have a **nest egg** for retirement.*

- **egg someone on:** to encourage someone to do something (that they probably shouldn't do!)
  *Fred was making jokes in class instead of listening to the teacher, and his friend kept **egging him on**. Stop it, you guys! Pay attention to the teacher!*

 JUST FOR FUN!

 Think about it: Which came first, the chicken or the egg?

 Here's a crazy picnic game called Egg and Spoon Race: Give each person a spoon, line up, put a **raw** egg in each spoon, and run! First one to the other side without dropping the egg is the winner. If you drop the egg—**YOKE**! (I mean YUCK! Haha!)

Jane and Sheila's Eggs-cellent (get it?) Egg Salad

Ingredients:

- 6 hard-boiled eggs, **chopped**
  (Don't forget to take the shells off!)
- **mayonnaise**
- chopped **celery**
- salt
- pepper

Directions:

Put it all in a bowl and gently mix together. Egg salad sandwiches are famous (and delicious), but we even like just a **scoop** of the yummy stuff with some crackers. (Oh boy. We're really getting hungry now . . .) Be creative! Some people like to add mustard or paprika. Some people like chopped onions. That's the best thing about cooking—you get to EGGS-periment! (Get it? Haha!)

VOCABULARY

- **adopt:** take something as your own
- **beads:** small, round decorative objects to make jewelry
- **boiled:** cooked in a pot of water
- **celery:** a long green vegetable often used in salads to add crunch and texture
- **chicks:** baby chickens (so cute!)
- **choke:** be unable to breathe because of an object caught in the throat
- **chopped:** cut into small pieces
- **conquered:** defeated; won against an enemy
- **costumes:** fun clothes worn to make you look like someone else
- **donate:** give
- **Easter Bunny:** that cute rabbit that hides the Easter eggs
- **egg hunts:** when children run around like crazy looking for plastic eggs with treats inside
- **elaborate:** with lots of details or decoration
- **fake:** not real

- **fasting:** not eating any food
- **feasting:** eating lots of food (we prefer this to fasting!)
- **floats:** large decorated flat trucks in a parade
- ⓘ **get it?:** do you understand the joke?
- **jelly beans:** yum! They're little bean-shaped, flavored soft candies in many colors
- **Lent:** a time period of sacrifice before Easter
- **look forward to:** be excited about something that you will do or that will happen soon
- **lunar:** based on the moon
- **Mardi Gras:** "fat Tuesday," the day before Lent begins; many celebrate with a big carnival
- **mask:** covers your face to make you look different
- **mayonnaise:** creamy white sauce made from egg yolks and oil.
- **observance:** a tradition or celebration; remembrance
- **omelet:** beaten eggs cooked in a pan until firm (we love cheese and ham mixed in!)
- **onlookers:** people watching something
- **over easy:** egg fried on one side, flipped over and BRIEFLY cooked on the other side so the yolk is still runny
- ⓘ **partygoers:** people attending fun events
- **pastry:** sweet baked breads; we love them!
- **plate:** the dish you put your food on
- **poached:** egg (no shell) cooked in water, still soft inside
- **poor:** having very little money
- **raw:** not cooked
- **resurrection:** coming back to life after death
- **sacrifice:** do something difficult
- **scoop:** large spoonful
- **scrambled:** beaten eggs stirred while being cooked
- **secular:** not religious
- **seder:** special traditional meal with customs to remember an important time in Jewish history
- **sunny side up:** egg fried on only one side so the yolk is still soft and bright yellow (like the *sun*)
- **trail:** a path to follow
- **yoke:** the bright yellow center of an egg
- ⓘ **yummy:** delicious

He: Hey, don't forget to print that report for the meeting this morning.

She: WHAT???? Wait, what report?

He: Wow, it's the one the boss asked you for . . . the sales report. We've got a meeting in an hour, and he needs it!

She: NO!!!! No, no, no, no! No, that report isn't **due** for a month . . . on the first.

He: My, my, my . . . Do you see the big 1 on the calendar? Today IS the first!

She: But wait! No, I thought the boss meant the first of NEXT month!

He: Hoo boy. NO, it's today and the big boss from headquarters is coming down just for our meeting.

She: Oh NO! What am I going to do? I haven't even started that report! The boss is going to kill me! Oh no. No, no, no, no, no, no . . . .

He: **Whoa!** Whoa*whoa*whoa*whoa* . . .

She: What?

He: Look carefully at the calendar. Yeah, it IS the first today, but it's the first of April . . . APRIL FOOL!

She: Oh man!!!!! Wow, you really **got me** that time! I was really in a **panic**!

He: Haha! I know! I was going to keep the joke going a little longer, but you really did look worried!

She: WORRIED?! No, that was PANIC!

He: Haha! Well, I guess I **got you back** for last year . . . Remember last April Fool's Day when you made me believe the boss was going to **fire** me?

She: Haha! Oh yeah . . . That really was a good one, wasn't it? Okay, I guess I deserved this, didn't I?

He: Um, yes. Yes you did!

She: Just you wait for next year . . .

TAKE A LOOK: Synonyms

You use them all the time. Every time you think about another way to say or write something, you're thinking about them. Yes, we're talking about synonyms! A synonym is a word with the same, or similar, meaning as another word. Using interesting synonyms makes your speech and writing more engaging. (See? *Engaging* is a synonym for *interesting*!) Look at the following sentences. Which one do you prefer?

- I'm hoping someone gives me a *big* diamond necklace for my birthday.
- I'm hoping someone gives me a *gigantic* diamond necklace for my birthday.

We know which one we like better! And, ahem, our birthdays are coming up soon . . .

YOUR TURN!

Read the sentences below. Find a synonym in the list that can replace the underlined word. Answers are on page 181.

_____	vacant	_____	cheerful
_____	prank	_____	starving
_____	odd	_____	huge
_____	colleagues	_____	mistake
_____	shut	_____	exit
_____	hilarious	_____	tasty

The new guy thought there was something (1) <u>strange</u> going on when he arrived at work. First, someone had (2) <u>closed</u> the front door of the office, when it was usually kept open. Then, when he went inside, none of his (3) <u>coworkers</u> were at their desks. In fact, the (4) <u>big</u> room was completely (5) <u>empty</u>. Wow! Had he made some kind of crazy (6) <u>error</u>? Was he coming to work on a weekend? He was so confused! As he turned toward the door to (7) <u>leave</u>, he heard, "APRIL FOOL!" and all of his coworkers jumped out! He really did feel like a fool. But it was all for fun, and his coworkers had prepared a (8) <u>delicious</u> breakfast for everyone to enjoy. This was a good thing because the new guy had forgotten to eat at home, and he was really

(9) <u>hungry</u>. Soon he saw the (10) <u>funny</u> side to their crazy (11) <u>trick</u>. Breakfast was a great start to the day, and everyone was (12) <u>happy</u> for the rest of the day (even the new guy!) thinking of their silly joke!

 APRIL FOOL'S DAY INFO TO KNOW:

 April Fool's Day (on April 1) is a silly holiday, just for fun. Play a trick on someone, but **watch out** for people **playing tricks** on you! It's a crazy day when everyone is suspicious of just about everything! Does someone want you to open a big box? Think about what might pop out! Is your friend offering you a special cookie? It's fine if it's not a plastic cookie! Don't get angry if someone plays a joke on you—it's just for fun. April 1 is one day of the year when everything that happens could be a trick!

In 1938, a radio show performed by Orson Welles frightened many people. It wasn't intended to trick people—it was a science fiction radio play. But people were fooled anyway.

The radio drama sounded like a real news report. It said that Martians had landed in New Jersey and were attacking. People believed it was true! There was panic everywhere.

Well, if we were alive in 1938, we wouldn't have panicked. If those Martians picked New Jersey to land, they were probably just looking for some decent tomatoes . . .

Here are a few tricks you could play:

- Put salt in the sugar bowl. That is NOT how you like your coffee! *Eeeew!*
- Set someone's alarm clock two hours early. (But not if you sleep in the same room; then the joke's on you, too!)
- Hide a plastic spider in the cookie jar.
- **Superglue** a dollar bill to the ground and watch people try and pick it up. We love that one!
- Carefully open a friend's bag of chips, empty out the contents, and replace with something different. Reseal the bag. Laugh when your friend opens the bag and you see his look of surprise!

Abracadabra! Alakazam!
Learn to do magic
And amaze the whole fam!

YOUR TURN!

Yes, everyone loves a good magic trick. If you can learn even one fancy card trick, your whole fam (family)—and even the kid next door!—will think you are an AMAZING *magician*! For your first trick, try to match the trick words to the picture. Answers are on page 182.

1. _____ magician's hat
2. _____ pull a rabbit out of a hat
3. _____ magic wand
4. _____ **saw** someone in half
5. _____ magic rings
6. _____ make flowers appear in the air
7. _____ a string of **handkerchiefs**
8. _____ glove

Are you thinking of learning some card tricks to amaze your friends? Your first trick is to learn some card vocabulary!

A **deck** is made up of 52 cards, divided into four **suits: spades, clubs, hearts,** and **diamonds**. Each suit has three picture cards: a king, a queen, and a **jack**.

The **ace** is usually the highest value card. The deck also contains two **jokers** (funny guys). When you start your card trick, it's important to **shuffle** the cards before you **deal** them.

Don't worry. If your magic tricks don't work, you can always just play cards. **Crazy Eights**, anyone?

FUN WITH IDIOMATIC EXPRESSIONS: Laugh like a fool!

- **act like a fool:** behave in a silly way
*You've got to stop **acting like a fool** in class and get more serious about your studies!*

- **you could have fooled me:** It would be easy to think the opposite
She: Did you know that new guy is really rich?
*He: **You could have fooled me!** Look at that broken old car he drives!*

- **make a fool of someone:** make someone feel embarrassed
*She really **made a fool** of that guy. He told his friends that she was **madly in love** with him, but she completely ignored him at the party.*

- **don't make me laugh:** that's ridiculous; I can't believe it
She: Hey, did you hear that the new guy asked for a big pay raise at work?
*He: **Don't make me laugh!** He never finishes his work, and he's always late!*

- **a laugh a minute:** lots of fun
*I'm so glad the new girl in the office sits near me. She's **a laugh a minute** with all her crazy stories and jokes.*

- **die laughing:** to laugh so much you can hardly catch your breath.
*That movie was so funny I thought I would **die laughing!***

JUST FOR FUN!

So you think you'd like to be a magician? This card trick sounds, um, tricky, but once you practice it a few times, it's easy. Make sure you know these expressions first.

Face up:    Face down:

1. Hold a deck of cards in your hand, *face down*.
2. Spread out the cards like a fan.
3. Tell a friend to take a card from anywhere in the deck.
4. Say, "Look at the card, but DON'T show it to me!"
5. **Cut the deck of cards** in half (still *face down*).
6. Tell your friend to put back her card in the cut deck.
7. Replace the top half of the deck.
8. Take the cards in order, one by one, and turn them *face up* on the table.
9. When you come to your friend's card, hold it up.
10. Watch the look of amazement on your friend's face.

But how did you know which card your friend had?

Remember when you cut the deck in half? At that point you need to take a quick look at the card above the place where your friend will put her card.

As you are putting the cards on the table, one by one, watch for that card. Your friend's card will be the next one you put down!

Haha! MAGIC!

VOCABULARY

- **ace:** highest card in a deck of cards; has the letter A in the corner
- **clubs:** one of four suits in a deck of cards, with a black clover design (You may also know a *club* is the wild place you go for dancing and fun!)
- **crazy eights:** a fun card game
- **cut a deck of cards:** divide the deck approximately in half
- **deal:** give cards out to each player of a card game
- **deck:** pack or set of cards
- **diamonds:** one of four suits in a deck of cards; has red, um, yes, diamond shapes.
- **due:** needed now
- **fire:** take away someone's job
- ⓘ **got me:** tricked me
- ⓘ **got you back:** tricked you as revenge!
- **handkerchiefs:** small pieces of silky cloth used by a magician in magic tricks; before the magic of tissues (!), people carried handkerchiefs for sneezing and cold symptoms.
- **hearts:** one of four suits in a deck of cards with red, um, yes, heart shapes
- **jack:** the young guy on one of the picture cards in each suit of cards
- **joker:** there are two of these funny guys in each deck of cards
- **madly in love:** really, really, *really* in love with someone
- **panic:** a feeling of being really, really worried, frightened, and nervous
- **playing tricks:** playing practical jokes
- **saw:** cut with a huge knife-like tool; also the name of the tool!
- **shuffle:** mix a deck of cards
- **spades:** one of four suits in a deck of cards; symbols on cards are black leaf shapes
- **suits:** the four design groups in a deck of cards. (You may know a suit as a matching set of clothes, too!)
- **superglue:** very strong glue; don't get it on your fingers, or you'll be stuck permanently to the next thing you touch!
- ⓘ **watch out:** be careful!
- ⓘ **whoa:** wait! hold on! calm down!

CINCO DE MAYO

There's another really fun spring holiday that's impossible to forget. Why is it impossible to forget? Because the name of the holiday is the DATE of the holiday! Yes, we're talking about Cinco de Mayo, which means . . . . May 5 in Spanish! Can you guess when we celebrate this holiday? Did you guess May 5?

Haha! We know what you're thinking: Why are we talking about a Spanish holiday? (Here's why: Because we love the food! And because, hey, we celebrate any holiday from anywhere!) Cinco de Mayo actually celebrates the long-ago **victory** of a small Mexican town against **powerful** French **forces**. Today it's a celebration of Mexican heritage in the U.S. with fabulous **ethnic** foods and fun. You'll see people wearing **sombreros**, breaking **piñatas**, dancing to great Mexican music, eating Mexican food like tacos, and just having a fabulous time! Here's the Spanish word for *party* that most Americans know: FIESTA!

TAKE A LOOK: Antonyms

An antonym is a word with an opposite meaning. We kind of like antonyms because they remind us of when we were kids and our moms used to say, "Why do you always do exactly the OPPOSITE of what I ask you to do?" Haha.

YOUR TURN!

Take a look at the following sentences. Decide which of the underlined antonyms makes better sense. See, Mom? We really *can* do what we're supposed to do! Answers are on page 182.

She: Hey, can you help me figure out what to do with the piñata for the Cinco de Mayo party?

He: Sure, where do you want to put it? I'm not sure about the weather today . . . It looks kind of (1) sunny/cloudy. Do you think it may be a good idea to hang it (2) inside/outside, just in case it rains?

She: Yeah, I think that's a great idea. It does seem a little (3) <u>hot/cold</u>, and we don't want any of the little kiddies to get (4) <u>ill/well</u> being out in nasty weather. Let's just hang it in the corner over there.

He: Okay, yeah, that looks like a good spot.

She: Let's just be careful not to hang it too (5) <u>low/high</u>, or the kids won't be able to reach it!

He: Ha, if they can't reach it, do we get to keep all the candy inside? Anyway, all I know is I'll be staying out of the way! When those kids start swinging that stick around it can get pretty (6) <u>safe/dangerous</u>!

She: Haha! Yeah, and they get so excited and (7) <u>noisy/quiet</u> you may need ear plugs, too!

He: WOW this piñata is (8) <u>light/heavy</u>. There must be a LOT of candy inside.

She: YES! Of course! It has a ton of candy! What fun is a piñata without lots of candy? But it sure did end up being quite (9) <u>cheap/expensive</u>. Hey, I know it looks pretty (10) <u>easy/difficult</u> to break a piñata, but if it takes the kids too long, we might need to help them out. (And I want those chocolates!)

CINCO DE MAYO INFO TO KNOW:

 DIY! Make a piñata (see how on page 88), or save time and just buy one. (If you buy one, you can choose from animal shapes, butterflies, stars, and cartoon characters.)

 Visit a Mexican restaurant! You may see a **mariachi band**. If these musicians come to your table and start playing, they will expect a tip! Don't know what food to order? Well, it all tastes great to us, but see a sample menu below if you need some help.

We're not sure if it's because we're hungry (Does it seem like we're *always* hungry?) or because it's true, but one of our favorite parts of living in a multicultural country is getting to enjoy all the ethnic foods that are available. In honor of Cinco de Mayo, here are some of our favorite Mexican foods for you to try. (Well, unless you ARE Mexican of course. Then you've probably been cooking and eating these for years.) Hey—if these are your usual foods, please send us an invitation to the next family **feast**! Anyway, enjoy the menu, and enjoy your meal! Or, as they say in Mexico, *buen provecho*!

- **arroz:** rice
- **burrito:** a large tortilla stuffed with meat, beans, or rice
- **carne:** beef
- **chimichanga:** a burrito, but DEEP FRIED (How much better can it get?)
- **enchilada:** a stuffed tortilla baked in tomato sauce
- **fajitas:** Pile it yourself! You get a **stack** of tortillas, **sizzling** meat of your choice, onions, peppers, guacamole, sour cream, and other additions. You prepare them any way you want them.
- **guacamole:** a creamy spread made with **avocado** and other ingredients—so, so, sooooo good!
- **quesadillas:** tortillas stuffed with cheese, then pan-fried or baked
- **salsa:** a sauce made from chopped tomatoes, onions, and peppers . . . how **spicy** do you like it?
- **taco:** crispy or soft tortilla filled with meat. It's smaller than a burrito so you may need a few. (Or a lot!)
- **taquitos:** small tacos rolled up with meat, then fried
- **tortilla:** a flat, circle-shaped bread made from corn or flour

FUN WITH IDIOMATIC EXPRESSIONS: Party!

- **life of the party/party animal:** someone who loves parties and is a lot of fun
  *Alfredo is such a **party animal**! Last night he was the **life of the party** with his funny stories and jokes!*

- **throw a party:** plan and host a party
  *Hey, it's my husband's fiftieth birthday next week! I'm going to **throw a party**. Do you want to come?*

- **party pooper:** someone who does not like parties and makes everyone else unhappy.
  *I'm not going to invite her to a party again. She just sat in the corner and wouldn't speak to anyone. She was a real **party pooper**.*

- **the party's over:** when something good comes to an end
  *Spring break is over, and it's back to school, homework, and tests. Sorry, kids—**the party's over**!*

DIY (DO IT YOURSELF)

Can you do it? Come on, admit it. You've seen something beautiful or fun in a newspaper or magazine, and you thought, "Hey, I can do that!"

Sure you can! And there are thousands of websites, magazine articles, craft stores, and supermarket departments to help you. You're a DIYer! (a do-it-yourselfer!)

Lots of places will give you clear step-by-step instructions on how to accomplish a project yourself, along with a list of things you'll need and where you can get them. Have fun! DIY!

◀ **Now listen to Audio Track 12**
(transcript on page 209)

JUST FOR FUN!

 Make your own piñata!

Yes, you can do it yourself! It's a bit messy, but it's FUN! Here's how to DIY:

- Blow up a balloon and cover it with layers of *papier-mâché*.
- Leave a small space at the end so you can fill it with candy later.
- Repeat with several layers and let dry completely.
- Make holes, add a loop of string for hanging, then pop the balloon and remove it.
- Decorate, and add LOTS of wrapped candy.
- Hang, and watch the kids hit it with a stick until the candy spills out.
- *Keep an eye on* those crazy kids, or you'll end the party with a trip to the hospital emergency room!

*　　　*　　　*

Want an easier version? Even the smallest kids can make this one.

- Get some small paper bags (the kind you put a school lunch in).
- Let the kids decorate them with markers. Add candy.
- Hang up a string between two posts.
- Attach the bags to the string with **clothespins**.
- When the kids take turns to hit the bags, they'll come down easily (and save a lot of complaining).

VOCABULARY

- **avocado:** fruit with a creamy center and very dark green skin. Makes a great dip!
- **clothespin:** a small wooden clip to hang clothes on a line to dry
- **DIY:** Do It Yourself!
- **ethnic:** about a different cultural group
- **feast:** a HUGE meal with many different foods
- **forces:** soldiers in an army; military groups
- ⓘ **keep an eye on:** watch carefully
- **mariachi band:** a group of traditional Mexican musicians
- **papier-mâché:** paper mixed with special glue to make art projects (and a big mess!) Yes, it's a French expression used in English!
- **piñatas:** large paper containers filled with candy. Kids try to break them at parties.
- **powerful:** very strong
- **sizzling:** making the sound of meat on a really hot grill
- **sombreros:** big Mexican hats!
- **spicy:** flavored with peppers and peppery seasonings
- **stack:** pile; many things on top of each other
- **victory:** success in winning against an opponent or enemy

Answers start on page 182.

CULTURE

During which of these celebrations would you hear people say the following? Fill in the blanks. Some choices may be used more than once.

April Fool's Day	Mardi Gras	St. Patrick's Day
Cinco de Mayo	Passover	
Easter	Ramadan	

1. I love listening to Dad's stories at the seder.
    _____

2. Quick! Try to catch some of the treats they are throwing from the floats!
    _____

3. Mom, I'm going to make some traps this year to see if I can catch that leprechaun. Then we can use his gold to take that trip to Hawaii you're always talking about! _____

4. OUCH! I nearly cracked a tooth! What IS that inside my cake? A tiny plastic baby? _____

5. Haha! I tricked you! You should have seen your face!
    _____

6. WOW, look at all those colored eggs! Let's see who can get the most.
    _____

7. When the sun has set, we can break the fast.
    _____

8. Wave the stick a little harder! If you don't hit it harder, the candy won't come out! _____

9. Mom, when will the bunny come? _____

10. Those green cupcakes look a little weird, but they sure taste good!
    _____

VOCABULARY

Fill in the missing words from this unit. The first letter is there to help you remember!

11. L_____ are really cute insects AND they're good for my roses. They eat the bad bugs that kill my roses!

12. Wow, look at that guy wearing a m_____! Do you think he's about to rob the bank, or is he just on his way to a party?

13. My husband loves to go to New Orleans to see the p_____ at Mardi Gras.

14. Not me! I HATE to go to Mardi Gras because there are too many people! C_____ scare me!

15. The yummiest parts of Cinco de Mayo are the treats inside the p_____!

16. Aaa*choooo*! Gosh, there is so much p_____ in the air this spring, I feel like a sneezing machine!

17. Allergies! With all this sneezing, I always seem to be running out of t_____!

18. Hey, Mom, when are you going shopping? There's no food in the f_____ and I'm starving!

19. So you want to give your wife a birthday present? J_____ of any kind is always a good idea: a ring, earrings, a bracelet. You get the idea!

20. All kids love a brightly colored b_____! Well, that is until it POPS or floats away! Then wait for the tears.

IDIOMATIC EXPRESSIONS

Look at the idiomatic expressions in these sentences. Can you remember what they mean?

21. Tony is *no spring chicken*, but he can still beat most guys half his age in soccer (at least in his dreams)!

22. Yikes! It seems like a new coffee shop *springs up* in this neighborhood every week. That's a lot of caffeine around here!

23. Our office is making a huge effort to *go green*. We're taking the stairs instead of the elevator, and we're recycling everything we can.

24. Haha! Look at that. My first time playing baseball and I hit the ball! **Beginner's luck!**

25. I have to be so careful what I say to my boss. She thinks I'm trying to get her job. Seriously, I feel as if I'm **walking on eggshells** half the time!

26. My friend is such a **good egg**; I was stuck in traffic, so she taught my class for me!

27. Don't make a **fool of yourself**! You just can't wear shorts and a T-shirt to your uncle's wedding.

28. My best friend is **a laugh a minute**; she's so much fun to go out with!

29. I'm going to **throw a party** for St. Patrick's Day. Let's invite everyone from our class.

30. But you can only come if you dance and have fun. No **party poopers** at my house!

SUMMER

SUMMER

IT'S A HEAT WAVE!

Oooh, baby, it's HOT HOT HOT!!!! I don't know about you, but we've been waiting for this season all year. Yay, summer! Breathe in the cool, **piney** mountain air! Taste the **tang** of the salty sea **breeze**! Listen to the little frogs, **croaking** near the lake... WAIT A MINUTE!...Those aren't frogs I hear! They're KIDS! Oh no! **School is out**, and so are the kids! Do you want to know what they're doing, now that there's no math homework? Haha! So do we!

When classes are not in session, we say, "School is out" or "There's no school."

◀ **Now listen to Audio Track 13**
(transcript on page 211)

Because most schools are closed, many Americans like to go **on vacation** during the summer. It's time to **pack up** the car, pack up the kids, and head to the mountains . . . or the beach . . . or the country. Places can get very crowded, so you may want to **book your stay** early in the year. And get ready for the **traffic**. Boo!

Yes, most of the traffic in the summer is usually going OUT of the city. This is good news if you want to visit museums and see the city sights! Cities are **pretty** quiet because lots of workers are home, packing everything up for vacation!

In the mountains, people can **camp out**, sleep under the stars, and listen to the **buzz** and chirp of **nighttime** bugs... (Hmm. As long as it's not the

It's BASEBALL SEASON! Sing along with us: *"Take me out to the ballgame, take me out with the crowd . . ."* Yes, the **pros** are playing the all-American sport in ballparks all over the country. Dads (and moms!) share tradition (and hot dogs!) with their kids as they all cheer for the **home team**. Let's go, Mets!

◀ **Now listen to Audio Track 14** (transcript on page 211)

crunch and munch of a bear eating lunch . . . OUR lunch!) At the beach, **sun-worshippers** use **beach chairs** and **beach towels** to relax. (Don't forget the **sunscreen**!) Grown-ups have their **beach books**, and the kids have their **summer reading**. (Ha, we hope so!) Everyone likes to **splash** in the **waves**, play **volleyball**, and make **sandcastles** with **pails** and **shovels** . . . Wow, and if there are fireworks at night, it's a perfect summer day!

Staying home during the summer is fun too. (Okay. Maybe it's not so much fun for poor Dad. He's out in the sun, **sweating** as he mows the lawn. Did we mention that it's HOT, HOT, HOT?!) In cities, kids play **street games**. There's handball, stickball, stoopball, and skully; hide-and-seek, hopscotch, jump rope and marbles. **Bored** kids **invented** these games, and let's just say this: most of them **involve** hitting a ball with a **stick**, or hiding, or running in the street. Don't ask us how to play. All we know is that it's **city-kid** fun!

A lot of families that don't **go away** for vacation plan special **day trips** to fun places: an **amusement park**, a **water park**, the zoo, or a museum. (Okay, we'll admit that the museum may be more fun for the parents than for the kids, ha.) And if the kids get tired of all those crazy **rides**, the family can **catch up on** the summer's **blockbuster** movies.

Even a trip for an **ice cream cone** (Oooh—how about two **scoops**? With sprinkles!) makes a hot day special. (Hey! Can we have a **sundae**, please? Extra **whipped cream**!)

When the summer is **in full swing**, the kids may start to get **antsy**. "Mom, I'm bored. There's nothing to do." Ha, but if parents suggest, "I have some **chores** you can do," **suddenly** the bored kids **disappear**! To keep kids busy

Do you have a favorite TV show? Forget it during the summer! The bad news is that summer is TV rerun season. Your favorite shows are on hiatus. A hiatus is kind of a vacation for TV shows. Television networks will rerun (show again) old episodes until the new season starts in September. (Boo! We've seen those old shows already!)

with fun and educational activities, a lot of families choose **summer camp**. Some **prefer day camp**, where kids spend a few hours each day doing fun activities. Parents **drop off** the kids in the morning, and **pick** them **up** in the afternoon. Some families choose **sleep-away camp**, where the kids will stay for a week or more. For a lot of kids, sleep-away camp is their first taste of **independence**. It can be exciting and fun, but some kids get **homesick** and can't wait for a letter or **care package** from home.

You've seen it in the movies. You've seen it on TV—the typical American favorite summer job! Cute little kids sit at a lemonade stand —a little table where they sell cups of lemonade for a few pennies. Lots of drivers will stop with a big smile and pay a dollar. Wow, look, Mom—I'm rich!

◀ **Now listen to Audio Track 15**
(transcript on page 212)

Summer camp is so big in the U.S. that you can find a camp for any child's interests. **Traditional** camps emphasize the **outdoors**, with fishing and swimming in lakes, sleeping in **tents**, and toasting marshmallows over a **campfire**. No city-kid street games here! There are sports camps, where kids practice soccer or tennis or skiing or baseball. There are **academic** camps that emphasize reading and math and preparation for big tests. There are arts camps for painting and theater and dance. There are computer camps, religious camps, camps for kids with **special needs** . . . even camps for **weight loss**! (Oh boy! Sign us up for that one.) In fact, if you can imagine an activity, you can find a camp with that **theme**. (HEY! Is there a "**Cupcake** Camp"? We want to go to camp and eat cupcakes! Then we'll go to the weight loss camp . . .) Bye-bye, kids! Have fun!

But summer **isn't all fun and games**. Many **teenagers** try to find **summer jobs**. It's hard work, but **teens** can earn some **pocket money**, or save for something special. If a house doesn't have **AC**, summer heat can be very uncomfortable. For **elderly** people, a heat wave can be **life-threatening**. It's important for everyone to stay **hydrated** by drinking **plenty** of water, and to avoid **strenuous** activity in the heat. **Check on** those older neighbors. **Make sure** everyone is keeping cool.

June is a busy month. The warmer weather means lots of June brides are hoping for sunny wedding days. Kids are graduating from high school or college. And let's not forget dear old Dad! Happy Father's Day, Dad! Thanks for all the hours in the backyard teaching me how to hit and catch a baseball!

TAKE A LOOK: Compound Words

What's better than one word? How about one word made out of two words?! It's like a magic trick! Let's see . . . hmm . . . . I want to *check* my *spelling*. Poof: **spell-check**! "Spell-check" is one word . . . (one very, *very* helpful compound word) that is formed by joining two words. (We know YOU don't need to use spell-check. We know YOUR spelling is perfect!)

A compound word is a new word made when you put two other words together. Often the two words are joined together with no space between: *base + ball = baseball*. Sometimes there's a hyphen (-) between them: *sun* + worshipper = *sun-worshipper*. And sometimes the two words stay separate: *ice + cream = ice cream*. Yes, we know what you're thinking: "How the heck can I figure it out?" When in doubt—dictionary! (But, haha, just to make it more complicated, sometimes different dictionaries say different things. That's crazy English for you.)

There are lots of fun summer compound words. Find these in the readings. Can you think of some others?

- ice cream
- sunscreen
- sandcastles
- homesick
- watermelon
- life-threatening
- **flip-flops**
- water park
- heat wave
- pocket money

YOUR TURN!

Complete the sentences with the best compound word from the list above. Answers are on page 184.

1. The kids were excited to go away to camp, but after a week they were _____, and they just wanted to see Mom.

2. Whew! The city's having a _____; the temperature is near 100° every day! Thank goodness for the AC . . . . but we're not looking forward to the electric bill!

3. Check on the neighbors. Very hot weather can be
   _____ to older people.

4. My favorite part of summer is wearing these comfortable
   _____. They're noisy, but they're comfy!

5. There are lots of exciting rides, and water is splashing everywhere—It's a
   fun day at the _____.

6. I think somebody forgot the _____. That sunburn will hurt
   tomorrow!

7. After Dad mowed the lawn, he relaxed under a tree and ate some cool,
   juicy _____.

8. Mmm! There's nothing better than some yummy
   _____ on a hot day. Better eat it quickly before it
   melts!

9. The kids had fun on the beach building
   _____ with their pails and
   shovels.

10. Sugar + lemon juice + water = lemonade.
    Lemonade + lemonade stand = _____ for the kids
    to spend!

VOCABULARY

- ⓘ **AC: Air Conditioning;** the system that makes your house cool in very hot
  weather
- **academic:** about school or education
- ⓘ **a lot/a lot of/lots of:** many, much
- **amusement park:** a place with CRAZY rides and fun games
- ⓘ **antsy:** unable to sit still; nervous
- **beach book:** a fun book to read at the beach; a book that doesn't need
  too much focus
- **beach chair:** a special low seat for sitting in the sand. It's light and easy
  to carry.
- **beach towel:** an extra large towel for drying off at the beach or for
  sitting on at the beach
- ⓘ **blockbuster:** a really, *really* successful movie that everyone wants to
  see!
- ⓘ **book a stay:** reserve a vacation place

- **bored:** *ho hum; Y A W N*; not excited.
- **breeze:** a light, gentle wind; also ⓘ something really, really easy!
- **buzz:** the humming sound a bee makes. Like this: *bzzzzzzzzzzzz*
- **campfire:** small outside fire made from twigs (small branches) of trees
- **camp out:** sleep outside in a tent or other shelter
- ⓘ **care package:** a surprise package of fun treats for someone who is away from home
- ⓘ **catch up on:** do, see, or learn about things you didn't have time to do before
- **check:** look
- ⓘ **check on:** (someone or something) look to see that someone or something is okay
- **chores:** jobs done around the house, like cleaning, washing dishes, etc.
- ⓘ **city kid:** a kid who grows up in the city
- **croaking:** the sound a frog makes. Come on! You know that sound! *rrrribbbbbit, rrrribbbbbit*
- **crunch:** the sound you make when you eat a potato chip!
- **cupcake:** a small cake, about the size of a . . . . say it with me . . . . CUP! (a CUPcake!)
- **day camp:** place where kids go for activities; they go home after a few hours each day
- **day trip:** going to a fun place for the day
- **disappear:** become invisible (impossible to see)!
- ⓘ **drop off:** bring someone to a place they need to go and leave him or her there
- **elderly:** older; people in their 70s or 80s
- **flip-flops:** those rubber summer shoes with a piece between the toes. They sound like *flippp floppp*.
- **go away:** go someplace for a time
- **homesick:** really, *really* missing home
- **home team:** the local team, playing baseball on its own baseball field
- **hydrated:** having enough water
- **ice cream cone:** a thin, crisp wafer shaped like a cone that holds ice cream. YUM!
- **independence:** acting alone and taking care of oneself with no help from others
- ⓘ **in full swing:** in the middle of lots of activity
- **invented:** created; made up

- **involve:** include or need (something)
- ⓘ **isn't all fun and games:** there are serious things to think about, too
- **life-threatening:** so dangerous that someone could die
- ⓘ **make sure:** check that something is right
- **munch:** eat something with a noisy sound
- **nighttime:** during the night
- **on vacation:** not at work
- **outdoors:** outside; wilderness: bugs and trees and animals and lakes and rivers and mountains and . . .
- ⓘ **pack up:** put all things you need together to go someplace
- **pail and shovel:** a container and digging tool (beach toys made of plastic)
- ⓘ **pick up:** get (someone) from a place
- **piney:** having the fresh smell of evergreen pine trees
- ⓘ **plenty:** a lot
- ⓘ **pocket money:** extra money to have for little expenses
- **prefer:** like better
- ⓘ **pretty:** quite, very; also beautiful
- **pros:** professional sports team players. They get paid!
- **rides:** attractions at an amusement park, like roller coasters
- **sandcastle:** a building made from sand at the beach
- ⓘ **school is out:** schools are closed
- **scoop:** a big spoonful serving of ice cream
- **sleep-away camp:** a place where kids go for activities; they stay there, usually for at least a week
- **special needs:** may need help with some everyday activities
- **spell-check:** what your device's spell-checker does! (It *checks* your *spelling*.)
- **splash:** make water move around . . . usually to get someone else wet!
- **stick:** a piece of wood, sometimes smooth like a bat
- **street games:** fun activities that use city streets and buildings as part of the game
- **strenuous:** very difficult; needing lots of strength
- **suddenly:** quickly, without notice
- **summer camp:** place with organized activities for kids
- **summer job:** a job, usually for teenagers, lasting a short time until they go back to school

- **summer reading:** books that teachers assign for kids to read during the summer
- ⓘ **sun-worshipper:** someone who likes sitting in the sun for a long time
- **sundae:** an ice cream treat with chocolate sauce, nuts, whipped cream, sprinkles . . . STOP US!
- **sunscreen:** a cream to prevent skin damage from the sun's rays
- **sweating:** perspiring; having drops come through your skin in hot weather
- **tang:** a strong taste or smell
- **teens:** see teenagers
- **teenagers:** kids from thir*teen* to nine*teen*
- **tents:** small shelters made from cloth for sleeping outside
- **theme:** the main idea
- **traditional:** usual; customary
- **traffic:** lots and lots . . . and *LOTS* of cars.
- **volleyball:** a game where people hit a ball over a net using their hands
- **water park:** an attraction with rides that go through lots of water
- **wave:** a big curve of ocean water; also move something quickly back and forth
- **weight loss:** lower body fat or weight; what you want when you go on a diet!
- **whipped cream:** sweet cream made into a fluffy, delicious cloud!

MEMORIAL DAY WEEKEND ◀ Now listen to Audio Track 16
(transcript below and on page 213)

Guy: Hey Lana, **what's with** the beach towel and flip-flops?

Girl: Are you kidding? Don't you know what weekend this is?!

Guy: Ummm . . . .

Girl: **Come on** . . . . Think about it . . . Monday is the last Monday of May. Does that ring a bell?

Guy: Ummm . . . .

Girl: Last Monday in May . . . .? Three-day **weekend** . . . ? Flags . . . ? Parades . . . .? No school. No work . . .

Guy: Wait! I've got it! It's Memorial Day Weekend! Wow, how could I forget that? My grandfather **served in the military**, and he died in battle. Of course I remember Memorial Day. I'm so proud that everyone takes a day to **honor** those who died for our country.

Girl: I knew you wouldn't forget such an important **national holiday**.

Guy: Of course not! In fact, I'm going to the **cemetery** with some **volunteers**. We'll put American flags on the **graves** of people who died fighting for our country in war. I'm proud to remember them.

Girl: Yes, and then we can watch the parade in town. I'm ready to wave the **Stars and Stripes**!

Guy: Yeah, but what about the beach towel and flip-flops . . . ?

Girl: Ummm . . . . Memorial Day is a holiday of **remembrance** . . . but it's also the **unofficial** FIRST DAY OF SUMMER!

Guy: Oh boy. I guess that means **traffic jams** on the **turnpike**. Oh well, SUNNYSIDE BEACH, HERE WE COME!

Girl: Hmm. Yeah. Us . . . . . . and three million other people.

TAKE A LOOK: *For* and *Since* with Time

For and *since* are tricky words to use when talking about time. When you mean a period of time, use *for*. When you mean a point in time, use *since*.

Example sentences:
*They have been working on the project **for** two weeks. (a period of time—two weeks.)*
*They have been working on the project **since** last Thursday. (It started at a point in time—last Thursday.)*

YOUR TURN!

See if you can figure out if *for* or *since* is needed in each of these sentences. Answers are on page 184.

1. Memorial Day weekend lasts _____ three long, lovely days.

2. Noooo! We've been stuck in traffic _____ 5:00 this morning!

3. Can you believe we've been going to Highland Lake every year _____ 25 years?

4. Uh-oh. She fell asleep in the sun _____ two hours. SUNBURN!

5. The kids have been building sandcastles _____ they arrived at the beach.

6. There is going to be a huge parade in town that will last _____ two hours.

7. Later we're going to the beach, and I've been making snacks _____ 6 a.m.!

8. I hope we don't get stuck _____ hours in the traffic.

9. We've been going to the same beach every Memorial Day _____ 2008.

10. Susanna has been counting the days until summer _____ New Year's Day!

11. The meat has been on the grill _____ a long time. It must be ready now!

12. I'm hoping my grandparents will come to visit _____ Memorial Day weekend.

 MEMORIAL DAY INFO TO KNOW:

Summer doesn't really begin until June, but because Memorial Day is part of a **long weekend**, many people think of it as the start of summer. V.A.C.A.T.I.O.N! Yay! You may be invited to a friend's house for a **cookout**. This is a very **casual** party. Wear casual, comfortable clothes, like jeans or shorts and a T-shirt.

The **host** will probably have plenty of food and **beverages**, but it's **polite** to ask if you can bring something. Maybe your friend will ask you to bring a salad or **side dish** to share. But even if he says no, most **guests** don't like to arrive at a party **empty-handed**. You can bring something sweet, or you can bring flowers or a bottle of wine.

 The gift that a guest brings to a party or dinner is called a *hostess gift*. It's not customary to bring a hostess gift if the party is just organized by a group—for example, classmates getting together on a weekend.

Your friend will probably **grill** simple, casual food. There may be special flag **decorations**, and **party plates** and napkins. Don't be surprised if your friend is wearing an **apron** with a funny **saying**, like "Kiss the Cook!" I don't want to kiss the cook, but I sure am getting hungry! Have fun at the **barbecue**!

 Pick your own farms are fun (and delicious)! In summer, peaches, strawberries, and lots of other kinds of fruit are ripe. Go to the farm and bring a large container to fill, or use a box that the farm provides (for a small **charge**). Go into the fields and pick the best fruit! (Snacking while you pick is the best part.) When you're finished, someone will weigh your fruit. Pay, then bring home your juicy, delicious dessert! Farm fresh!

YOUR TURN!

Are you enjoying your day at the beach? Did you pack everything you need? See how many fun-in-the-sun words you already know! You've seen all of these things! Each picture is part of a summer activity. Can you match the words to the picture? Answers are on page 185.

1. _____ sunglasses

2. _____ pail and shovel

3. _____ tube for swimming

4. _____ surfboard

5. _____ beach ball

6. _____ beach towel

7. _____ ice cream cone

8. _____ sunscreen

9. _____ flippers, mask, and snorkel (for looking under water)

10. _____ flip-flops

11. _____ sun umbrella

12. _____ ice pop

13. _____ beach chair (sand chair)

14. _____ sailboat

FUN WITH IDIOMATIC EXPRESSIONS: Summer!

- **it's a breeze:** it's really easy
  *She was really worried about the English test, but her friend said, "Relax! **It's a breeze!**"*

- **shoot the breeze:** talk about things that are not important
  *After the English test, the students sat outside, eating snacks and **shooting the breeze**.*

- **something fishy:** not right, suspicious; feeling distrustful about something; thinking that something bad is happening
  *Marco felt there was **something fishy** about the e-mail, so he did not click the link.*

- **no sweat:** easy!
  *Yolanda worried about the English exam, but it was easy. When Marco asked about the test, Yolanda replied, "It was everything we talked about in class. **No sweat!**"*

- **make a splash:** get a lot of special attention about something
  *Leo really **made a splash** when he threw lots of candy to the kids watching the parade.*

JUST FOR FUN!

 Kids love playing in the sand at the beach. Guess what? So do grown-ups! Some beaches have sandcastle contests during the summer. People make **fancy** buildings using beach sand and water, and they can win prizes. **Believe it or not**, there are actually professional sandcastle builders who travel to beach towns for the contests. The sandcastle **structures** and other fun designs are fun to see, but if a big wave comes in . . . **LOOK OUT**!

 Summer camp! The most famous treats that kids learn to make at camp are s'mores. Yes, it's a **wacky** name, but once you eat one, you'll be asking for some more *(s'more*, Get it? Haha!) You can make them, too, but save one for us! First, you need a campfire. (Be sure to do this only in your backyard or at a park where it's allowed.) *Shhhh!* Here's our secret s'mores **recipe**:

Jane and Sheila's Secret S'mores

Ingredients:

- **graham crackers**
- large marshmallows
- a chocolate bar

Directions:

- Put a marshmallow on a long stick. Hold it over the fire (carefully!) until the marshmallow is a nice golden brown color. (It will be deliciously **gooey** inside!)
- Break the graham cracker into two halves.
- Put half of the chocolate bar onto one half of the cracker.
- Put the marshmallow in the middle, and then cover with the other graham cracker half.

YUM!

(Hey, you can make these in your microwave, too, but that's no fun!)

VOCABULARY

- **apron:** something you wear over the front of your clothes to keep them clean while you cook
- **barbecue:** a cookout
- ⓘ **believe it or not:** "it sounds strange, but it's true!"
- **beverages:** drinks
- **casual:** informal; relaxed
- **cemetery:** the special area where people are buried when they die
- **charge:** cost
- ⓘ **come on!:** tell the truth! (also, hurry up!)
- **cookout:** a barbecue; a small party with food cooked outside
- **dish:** food item at a meal
- ⓘ **empty-handed:** without something to give the host
- ⓘ **fancy:** special and extra nice
- ⓘ **gooey:** soft and a little wet or sticky
- **graham crackers:** sweet, flat, rectangular cookies
- **grave:** place in the ground of a cemetery where people are buried when they die
- **grill:** cook outside
- **guests:** people invited to a party
- **honor:** show respect
- **host:** the person who has a party and invites friends
- ⓘ **long weekend:** a three-day weekend with a holiday on the Friday before, or the Monday after (Yay!)
- ⓘ **look out!:** Wow! Be careful!
- **national holiday:** an official government holiday; also *federal holiday*
- **party plates:** usually paper or plastic dishes that you throw away after using
- **pick your own:** choose your fruit or vegetables right where they grow on a farm or in an orchard.
- **polite:** the correct way to do something in a social situation
- **recipe:** instructions for cooking something
- **remembrance:** thinking about people who have died
- **saying:** a phrase that is funny or thoughtful
- **served in the military:** was part of the armed forces of a country
- **side dish:** small amount of food you've prepared as an extra choice
- **Stars and Stripes:** nickname for the American flag

- **structures:** things that are built
- **traffic jam:** lots and lots of cars not moving on a road or highway. *AAAARGH!*
- **turnpike:** a wide road with many lanes for traveling, usually at a fast speed
- **unofficial:** not formally approved
- **volunteers:** people who do something good for no pay
- ⓘ **wacky:** silly or crazy in a fun way
- **weekend:** Saturday and Sunday! (no work!)
- ⓘ **what's with:** "why do you have . . . "

INDEPENDENCE DAY / FOURTH OF JULY

Whoosh! BOOM! KABAAM! If the skies seem to be **exploding**, and your **pet** is hiding under the bed, it can mean only one thing: It's the Fourth of July! Independence Day is certainly the loudest American holiday. ☺

But first, a little history... **Quick**, think! Who's your **best friend**?

Today, one of this country's best friends is the United Kingdom. But it wasn't always so. The first American states were **colonies ruled** by Great Britain. People came to the 13 colonies for different reasons: to practice their religion freely, to **escape** from government rules so people could **make money** and keep it as they wanted, or because people were given land here as a gift. **Eventually**, people living in the colonies decided that they did not want to be **governed** by Great Britain. **Colonists** didn't want to pay taxes to a king more than 3,000 miles away, and they were not happy to have British soldiers living in the land.

Speaking of taxes . . . the Fourth of July is not a big holiday for going out to restaurants because everyone is in the backyard having a cookout! But if you do go out to eat, here's a tipping reminder: The usual tip amount is 15 to 20 percent. When you calculate the tip for the server, you do not include the tax in the total amount. (But the waiter will be very happy to have the extra cash if you forget. Haha!)

Some people in the colonies decided to **break the** king's **laws**, so the king sent even more soldiers! Fighting began between the king's soldiers and the colonists. Do you see where this is going? This is not going to have a **happy ending** for somebody!

The colonies joined together to fight against Great Britain and the British soldiers. This was the American Revolutionary War. It was a hard time. Many people were killed in the battles of the war. But on July 4, 1776, some **well-respected** leaders from the 13 colonies met in Philadelphia, Pennsylvania. They wrote one of the most important **documents** in U.S. history: the **Declaration of Independence**. The Revolutionary War became the fight for the new United States of America. The revolution was now an American War of Independence. This new country would now rule itself and be independent of Great Britain.

 INFO TO KNOW:

 John Hancock may be the most famous signer of the Declaration of Independence. People even use his name instead of the word "signature." They may say, "Just put your John Hancock on the line." Hancock signed the document in HUGE letters. One fun story is that he said, "Haha! Now King George can see it even without his reading glasses!" Is it true? We weren't there (come on . . . we're not that old), but we like the story!

We're glad to be friends again, Britain!
And Happy Birthday, USA!

Yes, the Fourth of July is a *really* big birthday party! And like any good party, the celebrating starts early and ends late. It's a national holiday. You'll see flags and red, white, and blue decorations everywhere. Yes, you'll even see red, white, and blue food! Towns will have parades, and people will have picnics. If the Fourth **falls on** a weekend, the federal holiday is observed on Friday or Monday, so it's another long weekend!

Wow! You think those colonists had problems? How about us modern Americans? Is it the *United Kingdom*? *Great Britain*? *England*? Are they all the same country? *AAACKKKK!!!*

Our British source tells us that technically the *United Kingdom* (*UK*) includes England, Scotland, Wales, and Northern Ireland.

Great Britain is England, Wales, and Scotland.

Britain is England and Wales.

WHOA, will there be a test?!

We're not the only ones confused. Our British source also tells us that most people in Britain . . . I mean Great Britain . . . I mean the United Kingdom . . . use all of them to mean the same country. *Whew!*

And, of course, it's time again for grilling outside: **hot dogs** and **burgers**! Baked beans and **home-made potato salad**! **Corn on the cob**! Ice cream and **pie**! Wow, we Americans sure do love our cookouts! (Sometimes we even invite our British friends. Haha!) And when the food is finished and the skies get dark, it's time for the best part—fireworks! Cities and towns have **spectacular** shows. Exciting **explosions** of firecrackers light up the sky with brilliant **sparks** and **showers** of light in bright colors. People will "*ooh*" and "*aah*!" Kids will shout, "WOW! Did you see that one?" It's a perfect finish to a proud day of fun and food. Well, unless you're the poor little **pooch** hiding under the bed . . .

TAKE A LOOK: ONOMATOPOEIA

Onomatopoeia! Onomatopoeia! Onomatopoeia! (We just love to say it, ha!) And we thank the Greeks for this very entertaining word. You know what we're talking about—these are the words that ARE the sound. Whoosh! BOOM! *KABAAM!* are all examples of onomatopoeia. Ha, and don't forget those *flip-flops!*

YOUR TURN!

Say the words in the sound column out loud (Haha! Don't be surprised if you get some funny looks from people around you!) Can you figure out which thing makes each sound? Answers are on page 185.

Sounds:

a. buzz

b. BOOM!

c. sizzle

d. clink clink

e. splash!

f. HONK HONK!

g. *y a w n*

h. meow

i. quack quack!

j. tick, tock

k. *zoom!!!!*

l. woof, woof, WOOF, WOOF!

1. _____ bacon in a frying pan. YUM!

2. _____ Charlotte jumping into the water

3. _____ an impatient driver in New York traffic

4. _____ your hungry cat . . . Hey, somebody feed me!

5. _____ a duck on a pond

6. _____ your neighbor's dog at 6 a.m.!

7. _____ a clock in a quiet room

8. _____ a bee in your garden

9. _____ Sheila's car on the turnpike. Hey, she's late!

10. _____ ice cubes in a glass

11. _____ a tired student during a boring lecture

12. _____ fireworks exploding

☑ FOURTH OF JULY INFO TO KNOW:

☑ Fireworks are the most exciting part of Fourth of July celebrations. But be careful! Many states have laws that say people can't have fireworks. In many places, the only **legal** way to enjoy fireworks is to see an official town or city **display**. Even if you come from a place that allows people to buy fireworks, don't bring them to a **backyard** party or **BBQ**! (They're dangerous. And they scare the pooches!) Instead, bring some nice picnic food to share. We vote for potato salad. Everyone loves it!

☑ Sometimes you may see the U.S. flag flying at half-staff (only halfway up the **flagpole**). Some people may call this at half-mast. It's a symbol of sadness and respect for an important person who has died. Only a government official can order that the flag be flown at half-staff.

☑ Do you know what the U.S. flag design means? The **stripes** (count them!) represent the 13 colonies that were the **foundation** of the country. The stars represent the states. Okay—quick quiz: How many stars are there in the flag? _____ Yes—50 stars for the 50 states! A **gold star** for you if you got it right!

 Okay, we know this sounds crazy, but some states have wacky rules. (We're looking at you, Pennsylvania!) Stores are allowed to sell big fireworks, but only to people who live out of state. HUH?

◀ **Now listen to Audio Track 17**
(transcript on page 214)

YOUR TURN!

Can you complete the sentences with the best words? Answers are on page 186.

1. The Fourth of July is also called _____.

2. The 13 American _____ of Britain decided not to pay taxes to the British king.

3. The _____ is one of the most important documents in American history.

4. For lots of people, the best part of the holiday is the _____ show at night.

5. **Do your homework!** In many states, it is not
_____ for people to have fireworks.

6. Bring a flag to wave as you watch the
_____ in your town.

7. Parks are popular places to have a _____. Bring lots of food! And friends!

8. We love our little animals! But the Fourth of July is a time when a lot of _____ find crazy places to hide from the loud noises. Check under the bed!

9. We fought a War of Independence against
_____, but it's now one of our best friends.

10. If you're lucky, a good friend will invite you to a fun
_____ in his or her backyard!

Okay, you did a great job, so here's another **top-secret** recipe:

Sheila and Jane's Perfect (and Popular!) Potato Salad

Ingredients:

- **about** 6 potatoes
- 3 Tbsp of rice vinegar
- about ¾ cup of mayonnaise
- about a cup of chopped celery
- 1 small onion, chopped
- a hard-boiled egg

Directions:

- Wash the potatoes, then cut into **chunks.**
- Put the potatoes in a pot of water. Heat on the stove until **boiling**, then **lower** the heat and cook until the potatoes are **tender**. This should take only about 10 minutes. Then drain all the water and let the potatoes **cool.**
- Mix all the other **stuff** in a bowl. Then add the potatoes.
- **Chill** in the fridge, put some pretty green leafy thing on top, and then take your potato salad to a picnic!

You know us—our idea of cooking is putting popcorn in the microwave. But if *you* actually cook (!), there are some very common recipe abbreviations to know:

- t or tsp = teaspoon
- T or Tbsp = tablespoon (Don't ask us why it has a capital "T"!)
- c = cup
- oz = ounce
- lb = pound (We know what you're thinking: Why L? Why B? Those letters aren't even in the word *pound*! It's just more Latin that we adopted in English.)

FUN WITH IDIOMATIC EXPRESSIONS: Picnic Fun!

- **Hot dog!:** an expression that shows someone is very excited about something. Wow!
  Hot dog! Erin was in Japan last week, but she's home now and she's coming to the cookout!

- **it's no picnic:** it's not easy; it's not fun
  *Lana has four small children, two jobs, and she's trying to learn English! **It's no picnic** being a working mom and student.*

- **red flag:** a warning that there's a problem
  *His résumé showed that he had six jobs in two years. Uh-oh. That will be a **red flag** to the hiring person.*

- **rain on someone's parade:** disappoint someone who is very excited by saying something bad about the situation
  *"I hate to **rain on your parade**, but the boss just canceled the great project you finished."*

- **flag down someone (or something):** wave, or signal, for someone to stop
  *When the rain started, Marco quickly tried to **flag down** a taxi. (Ha, good luck, Marco!)*

VOCABULARY

- ⓘ **about:** approximately; estimated
- • **backyard:** grassy area behind a house
- ⓘ **BBQ:** barbecue! (it's also okay in lowercase: bbq)

- **best friend:** a very special friend; in text language, your "bff" (best friend forever)
- **boiling:** so hot that bubbles form and move around
- **break the laws:** disobey rules of the government
- ⓘ **burger:** hamburger. Yum! cooked ground beef served on special bread (called *rolls*, or *buns*). *Mmmmm*. Make mine a *cheese*burger! With onions! (Oh boy, somebody stop me!)
- **chill:** make something cold
- ⓘ **chunk:** large piece
- **colonies:** lands under the control of a government far away
- **colonist:** someone who lives in a colony
- **cool:** not hot at all
- **corn on the cob:** YUM. Boil the whole ear (piece) of corn. Spread on butter and sprinkle with salt. (And invite me over!)
- **Declaration of Independence:** the historic document that announced a break with Great Britain for an *independent* United States of America.
- **display:** a show of something
- **document:** a very important paper
- ⓘ **do your homework:** get information before you do something or go somewhere
- **escape:** get safely away from something
- **eventually:** finally, after some time
- **exploding:** blasting with fire and noise
- **explosion:** a blast of fire and noise
- **falls on:** occurs on
- **flagpole:** the long post used to hold a flag
- **foundation:** basis; the start for something
- ⓘ **gold star:** special design that shows excellence
- **governed:** ruled by a government
- ⓘ **happy ending:** a result that is pleasing to everyone
- **home-made:** prepared at home, with fresh ingredients
- **hot dog:** another cookout meat (like a sausage), served on special long bread called a roll or bun
- **legal:** allowed by law
- **lower:** reduce; bring down
- ⓘ **make money:** earn money, as pay
- ⓘ **ooh and aah!:** "WOW!"

- **pet:** the animal you have at home that you love! (Mine is a dog. Hers is a cat.)
- **pie:** a dessert made from fruit baked inside a crust (a thin pastry)
- ⓘ **pooch:** dog
- **potato salad:** a common picnic food made of cooked potatoes and other ingredients. It's served cold.
- **quick:** fast
- **ruled:** governed
- **shower:** lots of small bits of something (light, or water, or sparks . . .
- **sparks:** small bits from a fire
- **spectacular:** AMAZING! FABULOUS!
- **stripe:** a long line of color on a piece of cloth
- ⓘ **stuff:** things; items
- **tender:** just a little soft
- **top secret:** really, really private . . . *shhhh!!!*
- **well respected:** trusted by many people for honorable work

WEDDINGS!

Here comes the bride!

Summer is popular for another type of celebration too—**marriage**! A wedding day is not an official holiday, but, haha, we bet there are plenty of **brides** who think it should be. Ah, **true love**! First comes "Will you marry me?" Then comes . . . . . CRAZY! Oh come on. **Admit it**! You know what we're talking about. **Popping the question** is the easy part!

We're pretty sure **planning** a wedding makes families everywhere a little crazy, but in the U.S. we have a special name for brides who **stress out** over the **details**: **Bridezilla**! Yes, this is a bride who turns into a **Godzilla**-monster if there is a problem. And, take it from us, there is *always* a problem. Once the Bridezilla **calms down**, the wedding is a happy time with beautiful traditions. And these traditions can be from all over the world in our **melting pot** country: **henna** designs on hands, **borhani** and tea-sharing **ceremonies**, **exchanging** flower garlands, special **veils** and dances, and our very favorite of all—feasting for DAYS! **Modern** couples choose old cultural customs or add special new ones, but like ceremonies everywhere, a typical American wedding is a day of celebration and **joy**.

As any Bridezilla can tell you, the perfect wedding means months and months of planning. First, a couple chooses the **date**. Then they decide on a **venue**. Will it be a religious ceremony? A simple **civil** ceremony in **City Hall**? (Wow! Try saying that last sentence three times, FAST. Now that's what we call pronunciation practice! Haha!) What about a **destination wedding**? Oh yeah, we love that one—we get to travel to an exciting place and watch our friends get married on the beach. (We hope the sand **crabs** don't think our toes are lunch!) How about this one—our brother had a **Vegas wedding**! He and his wife were married by an **Elvis impersonator**! *Elvis* married my brother! ELVIS!

 Marry . . . Now that's tricky! No, we're not talking about husband and wife—although that's pretty tricky, too. Haha! We're talking about the verb *marry*. We use it in a few ways:

1. It can mean performing the ceremony that joins two other people in a marriage. *(Elvis **married** Keith and Dawn.)*

2. And it can mean becoming joined as a spouse to someone in a marriage. *(Keith **married** Dawn in Las Vegas.)*

3. And just to keep it nice and tricky to learn . . . We often say "get married."
*(Keith and Dawn decided to **get married** in Las Vegas. A guy pretending to be Elvis **married** them. They **married** on a Tuesday in June.)*

It's hard to think of anything more exciting than Elvis, but shopping for a wedding dress is exciting, too. And crazy! The bride may **try on tons** of dresses before finding "the perfect one" that makes her feel like a princess. For good luck, it's tradition for the bride to wear "something old, something new; something **borrowed**, something blue." *Something old* could be a special piece of old jewelry from a grandmother. It symbolizes connecting the present and future family to the past **generations**. *Something new* could be the wedding dress . . . or wedding ring . . . or new shoes! It symbolizes success and a fresh start on a new life for the couple. *Something borrowed* could be a necklace or earrings borrowed from a happily married friend. It means that family and friends will **support** the new bride, and **share** their happiness with her. *Something blue* represents **faithfulness**, **loyalty** and love. Many brides **pin** a small blue ribbon to their dresses. But how about blue nail polish? How about blue shoes? Oh boy, how about BLUE HAIR?

Don't forget about the **bridal party**! The **groom** usually asks his brothers or close friends to be **ushers**. Their job is to **walk** the guests to their seats before the **ceremony**. The **bridesmaids** are family members or close friends of the bride. Their job is to try to **keep** the bride **from** becoming a

Bridezilla. Haha! The **maid of honor** and **best man** are usually special family members who are the official **witnesses** to the marriage.

Finally, when the **Big Day** arrives, the bride is ready to walk down the **aisle** in her beautiful white dress and veil. Traditionally, the bride's father walks her down the aisle. The most popular music for this is Richard Wagner's *Wedding March*, which is also known here as *Here Comes the Bride. Dah dah di daah . . . . dah dah di daaaah . . . .* (Sorry! Did we just write that? We're singing it in our heads!)

If the couple marries in a church, the groom will meet his new partner for life at the **altar**. Some couples may stand under a special covering called a **chuppah**. Some couples may exchange **crowns** or light a candle together. Some couples may **jump the broom**. Sometimes the groom will **smash** a glass. Each couple chooses its own special touches, but the most important part of the ceremony is when they exchange **wedding vows**. Listen to hear them say, "**I do**!" And then the famous words everyone has been waiting to hear: "I now pronounce you MARRIED." YAY! They did it!

Of course some couples decide to **skip** the craziness **altogether** and just **elope**. If a couple decides to elope, they usually keep it a secret. They want a quiet little ceremony without all the stress and expense. (WHAT? No stress? What kind of a wedding is that?) After the wedding and all the celebrating, the couple often takes a relaxing vacation. The newlyweds go off on their **honeymoon** . . . and talk about every wonderful minute of the wedding! (We're pretty sure they  forget all about the crazy planning while they're relaxing on the beach. ☺)

 Don't be surprised if you see a bag or box for cards and money at a wedding **reception**. Quite often guests give money as a wedding gift. Although every guest should send or bring a gift, it can be any gift you choose . . .

TAKE A LOOK: Abstract Nouns

Bride and *groom*. *Las Vegas*. *Wedding cake*. They're all nouns. (Hey, can you spot the separated compound nouns?) As you know, a noun is a person, place, or thing. An *abstract noun* is one that you can't see, hear, touch, taste, or smell. But it's still some*thing*! It's an idea or a feeling. It may be a quality that a person has. Take a look at some common abstract nouns below. Check a dictionary if you're not sure of the meaning.

Positive Abstract Nouns	Negative Abstract Nouns
friendship	anger
happiness	anxiety
joy	disbelief
love	loneliness
relief	fear
surprise	sadness
pride	worry
honesty	hate
creativity	nervousness

YOUR TURN!

Now read the following short story about a relationship (another **abstract noun**!). Choose words from the list above to best complete the sentences. Sometimes more than one answer is possible. Answers are on page 186.

All's Well That Ends Well

Pablo and Juanna had been good friends since they were kids. For years, they played together all the time. As they got older, they realized that their relationship was more than just a wonderful (1) _____. They started dating and soon realized their (2) _____ for each other. One bright, sunny day Pablo popped the question! He asked Juanna to be his wife. This was not a (3) _____ to their friends! They could see the (4) _____ in the couple's eyes. After much planning, the Big Day was about to arrive. The day before the wedding Juanna was full of (5) _____. She hoped that everything would go well, but mostly she hoped that she wouldn't trip on her dress walking down the aisle! Juanna's father smiled with (6) _____ as he walked next to his beautiful daughter. They made it to the altar without a dress disaster!

What a (7) _____! But soon that feeling turned to (8) _____ when Juanna's friend whispered that Pablo had lost the ring . . . LOST THE RING?! *Nooooo!* It can't be! Unbelievable! But Juanna took a deep breath. She realized that a wedding day is no day to be upset. After all, she looked at the funny side—Pablo used a pop-top ring from a soda can for the ceremony! A SODA CAN wedding ring! She had to admit that showed his (9) _____. Pablo and Juanna could choose another ring on their honeymoon. All the (10) _____ about wedding plans disappeared as the happy couple said, "I do." (But we're pretty sure Juanna won't forget about shopping for her new ring. ☺)

Trip is a noun! *Trip* is a verb!

"To take a trip" means to go to some place and return.

"To trip" is to hit your foot on something and fall.

*I was so excited about my **trip** to Italy that I ran to the departure gate and **tripped** over my suitcase. Bye-bye, **trip** to Italy.*

☑ WEDDING INFO TO KNOW:

 Weddings are usually very **dressy events**. Women should wear very nice party clothes. Men should wear a **suit**, or a jacket and tie. If a wedding is extra formal or very casual, the bride will write that on the **invitation**.

 Wedding invitations can be very fancy. Often they will contain a special **response card** and envelope for you to mail back to the person planning the wedding. On the card you should write your name and check *Yes, I will attend*, or *No, I will not attend*. This is important because the wedding planner must know how many chairs and tables will be needed, and how many meals to serve. Don't forget to mail the card back! It's **considered rude** not to **RSVP**. You don't want Bridezilla to get antsy, do you?

We have to admit it. There are some things that just sound a little fancier in another language! So we say, "Thank you, France, for RSVP!"

Americans use these letters on many special invitations. It's a way to ask guests to reply to the invitation. RSVP means "**r**épondez **s**'il **v**ous **p**laît"… please respond.

Some invitations may say in English, "The favor of a reply is requested," but we like RSVP!

◀ **Now listen to Audio Track 18**
(transcript on page 215)

Friends who are invited to a wedding should send a gift. The couple may have a **registry** with a list of gifts (in all **price ranges**) that they would like to receive. This is **practical** so the **newlyweds** don't get four **blenders** (haha!), but you should send (or bring) anything you choose. (If you order a gift online or by phone at a big **department store**, they can **gift-wrap** it beautifully and send it to the couple before the wedding day.)

The reception is a big happy party after the wedding, with food and dancing. Sometimes this is held in a special place just for weddings, and sometimes it may be in a nice resturant. No matter where it is held, at a typical reception, the bride will have a special dance with her father, and the groom will have a special dance with his mother. Then the bride and groom will have their first dance together. There will be a special toast to the newlyweds, the bride and groom will cut a **tiered** wedding cake, and all the guests will eat and dance. Hey, they forgot to invite us! Have FUN!

YOUR TURN!

Everyone loves a wedding! How many wedding words do you remember? Write the letter of the best meaning for each word. Answers are on page 186.

a. A marriage ceremony at a **faraway**, special place.

b. DO THIS! Let the bride know you're coming (or not) by sending back the response card!

c. What they say when asked if they want to marry each other!

d. The ceremony of getting married, with special customs and traditions.

e. The fun party after a wedding or other big event.

f. Words that offer good wishes to the newlyweds, often followed by champagne.

g. She's a friend who helps the bride with plans.

h. The lucky guy at the wedding

i. Get married secretly, without telling anyone. (No Bridezillas here!)

j. The legal joining of two people together as a couple

1. _____ wedding

2. _____ marriage

3. _____ bridesmaid

4. _____ groom

5. _____ elope

6. _____ destination wedding

7. _____ toast

8. _____ RSVP

9. _____ reception

10. _____ I do!

FUN WITH IDIOMATIC EXPRESSIONS: Falling in Love!

- **tie the knot:** get married!
  *They were in love, they spent most of their time together, and they wanted to start a family, so they decided to **tie the knot** in June.*

- **made for each other:** perfect partners; getting along very well
  *They loved to do the same things, and they laughed at the same silly jokes—**they were made for each other!***

- **have a crush (on someone):** to have romantic feelings for someone without really knowing them well
  *All the women in the office **had a crush on** the good-looking new guy in the office. Can we get you some coffee, new guy?*

- **a match made in heaven:** a perfect couple
  *Peggy and Russ just celebrated their 66th wedding anniversary. Now that's what we call a **match made in heaven!***

- **pop the question:** ask someone to marry you
  *After dating Lia for two years, Alan finally decided to **pop the question**. It's about time, Alan!*

WEDDING CUSTOMS AND SYMBOLS

First, a crazy joke:

Q. What do you call a fruit that can't get married?
A. A cantaloupe!

(Here's why it's funny: The melon called a *cantaloupe* is pronounced "can't elope." Get it? Haha!)

Oh, the crazy things we do! Here are some typical customs and symbols for a wedding day.

- **cutting the cake**—The new couple cuts the cake together to symbolize their new shared life.
- **Rain on your wedding day** means good luck!
- Ooh, but if the **groom sees the bride before the wedding**, it's bad luck!
- The **wedding ring** symbolizes the circle of love; it has no beginning and no end.
- The **wedding veil** tradition began with the ancient Romans and Greeks. They believed that a veil would protect the bride from **evil spirits**. (We think a Bridezilla will scare away all the spirits!)
- **throwing the bouquet**—At the end of the reception, the unmarried women gather together. The bride turns around so that she can't see the women, and then she throws her bouquet back. Whoever catches it will be the next one to get married!
- **shoes and cans on the newlyweds' car**—Sometimes friends of the couple tie old shoes to the back of the couple's car for good luck. (Really, we think they do it because it will drive the bride and groom crazy!)

We don't know about all these Greek and Roman evil spirits hanging around weddings, but we're sure glad we **figured out** how to scare them away!

VOCABULARY

- ⓘ **admit it!:** tell the truth!
- **aisle:** long passageway between seats
- **altar:** the table used for religious ceremonies, usually in a church
- **altogether:** completely
- **best man:** special person the groom picks to be his official witness to the marriage (often a brother or best friend)
- ⓘ **Big Day:** nickname for any important event
- **blenders:** electric appliances for mixing liquids
- **borhani:** a yogurt drink served at Bangladeshi weddings
- **borrow:** take or use something from someone else for a short time (then return it!)
- **bridal party:** the bride, groom, bridesmaids, and ushers
- **bride:** the woman getting married
- **bridesmaid:** a family member or friend of the bride who helps her with preparations
- ⓘ **Bridezilla:** a bride who becomes a monster because of TOO MUCH STRESS!
- ⓘ **calm down:** relax
- **ceremony:** an important ritual or event, with special traditions
- **chuppah:** a covering used in some wedding ceremonies
- **City Hall:** the building for government offices
- **civil:** governmental
- **considered:** thought
- **crabs:** small beach animals with a hard shell and claws. Ouch! Watch your toes!
- **crown:** special decoration of jewels or flowers that's worn on the head
- **date:** the day, month, and year
- **department store:** a large store that sells many types of items
- **destination wedding:** a wedding ceremony held in a faraway place. You must travel there to attend.
- **details:** arrangements for every part of an event
- ⓘ **dressy:** fancy; formal
- **elope:** marry quickly, in secret, without a big ceremony
- **Elvis:** Are you kidding?! You know this one! It's ELVIS! ELVIS PRESLEY! THE KING! THE KING OF ROCK 'N ROLL! Come on . . . E L V I S !!!
- **event:** important occasion

- **evil:** very, terribly bad
- **exchange:** give something to someone and receive the same kind of thing
- **faithfulness:** staying true to someone
- **faraway:** not near home; at a great distance
- **figured out:** find a solution to a problem
- **generation:** group of people of about the same age
- **gift-wrap:** special paper and decorations to make a gift look beautiful
- **Godzilla:** He's the famous huge lizard-like monster from the movies.
- **groom:** the man getting married!
- **henna:** a special dye or coloring used to make designs for special occasions in some cultures
- **honeymoon:** a vacation that a newlywed couple takes
- **I do!:** the words that mean, "YES! I will marry this person!"
- **impersonator:** someone who pretends to be someone else
- **invitation:** a card asking you to attend a party or other event
- **joy:** happiness
- **jump the broom:** stepping over a broom as a symbol; it's a special tradition for some people
- **keep (someone) from:** stop or prevent (someone) from doing something
- **loyalty:** staying true to a person or belief
- **maid of honor:** special person the bride picks to be her official witness to the marriage (often a sister or best friend)
- **marriage:** the act of becoming joined as a couple
- ⓘ **melting pot:** joining together of many different cultures in one place
- **modern:** up to date; of present times; having new ideas
- **newlyweds:** the couple who have just married!
- **pin:** attach with a small metal fastener; also the metal fastener!
- **plan:** think about and decide on what to do
- ⓘ **pop the question:** ask someone to marry you!
- **practical:** useful
- **price range:** costs from low to high or high to low
- **reception:** a special party, usually with food and drinks, after a wedding or other event
- **registry:** a file with a list of items
- **response card:** a small card or paper for you to say if you will attend the event

- **rude:** not polite; unacceptable
- **share:** enjoy together
- ⓘ **skip:** don't do; leave out; omit
- **smash:** break into lots of small pieces
- **spirit:** an invisible creature
- ⓘ **stress out:** become nervous and upset about something
- **suit:** clothes with matching pants (or skirt) and jacket
- **support:** help
- **tiers:** levels; layers of a cake
- **toast:** good wishes for the new couple, often with guests sharing champagne. Often, the wedding toast will tell stories about the bride and groom.
- **true love:** they're perfect for each other!
- **try on:** put on clothing to see if it fits (and looks perfect!)
- **usher:** the person who shows someone where to sit
- ⓘ **Vegas wedding:** usually a crazy, quick wedding in Las Vegas (often not planned in advance)
- **veil:** a piece of lace or light fabric covering someone's face
- **venue:** the place where an event takes place
- **walk:** escort; bring someone to his or her seat
- **wedding vow:** a promise made at the wedding by one partner to the other
- **witness:** someone who signs the official marriage document as a true event

CULTURE

Look at the following statements and decide if they are true or false. If they are false, change them to make them true.

1. _____ Memorial Day is when we say "thank you" to those who are serving in the military.

2. _____ Memorial Day weekend is the unofficial start of the summer.

3. _____ If you're invited to a cookout, it's nice to bring something, even if the host says it's not necessary.

4. _____ Independence Day is celebrated on July 4.

5. _____ Independence Day celebrates America's freedom from France.

6. _____ You can buy fireworks at local stores all over the U.S. to celebrate the holidays.

7. _____ The Document of Independence is the historic document that announced a break with Great Britain for an independent United States of America.

8. _____ The American flag has 50 stars for the 50 states, and 12 stripes for the 12 original colonies.

9. _____ It's traditional for a bride to wear something old, something new, something borrowed, and something blue on her wedding day.

10. _____ If you receive an invitation to a wedding but you cannot attend, it's not necessary to reply to the invitation.

VOCABULARY

Can you remember these nouns from the summer section? Write the letter next to the word that fits the definition.

a. a cream to prevent skin damage from the sun's rays

b. the person who walks you to your seat at a wedding

c. a really, really successful movie that everyone wants to see

d. a long passageway between sections of seats

e. someone who likes sitting in the sun for a long time

f. the vacation that a newlywed couple takes

g. the man getting married!

h. the woman getting married!

i. instructions for cooking something

j. a grassy area behind a house

11. _____ sun-worshipper

12. _____ sunscreen

13. _____ backyard

14. _____ usher

15. _____ bride

16. _____ groom

17. _____ recipe

18. _____ blockbuster

19. _____ aisle

20. _____ honeymoon

IDIOMATIC EXPRESSIONS

Can you put these idiomatic expressions into the sentences where they make sense?

shoot the breeze	tie the knot
something fishy	made for each other
it's no picnic	have a crush (on someone)
flag someone (or something) down	no sweat!
hot dog	make a splash

21. The police knew _____ was going on when they saw two guys climbing into the window of the bank.

22. The company really wanted to _____ and get people excited about the cool new product.

23. _____ working the night shift, especially with *my* neighbors. They are so noisy during the day when I'm trying to sleep.

24. Good luck trying to _____ a taxi in bad weather! Everybody wants one!

25. Cem and Zeynep have been dating for five years. I sure hope they _____ soon. I haven't been to a good wedding in a long time!

26. My parents were married for 54 years and they never had a fight. They were _____.

27. Don't worry! Soon you'll know everything there is to know about American culture._____!

28. When Sheila and Jane relax, they like to sit with a cup of coffee and _____. (Okay, maybe they eat donuts, too. Haha!)

29. _____ ! The boss LOVED my report, and now she's giving me a big promotion!

30. I think Toby _____ on Celia. He keeps finding reasons to walk past her desk.

AUTUMN/
FALL

AUTUMN/FALL

BACK TO SCHOOL!

"BOO!!!" say the kids. "YAY!!!" say the parents.

Oh boy, that can only mean one thing: It's **back to school**! Sorry, kids, but say good-bye to all that fun summer stuff, and say hello to homework and the **three Rs**! That big yellow school bus is on its way, and parents everywhere are **smiling from ear to ear**! **Sharpen** those pencils, kids!

In many places in the United States, school begins the day after Labor Day. This holiday is always on the first Monday in September. Although **fall** doesn't begin until September 22 or 23, many people think of Labor Day as the first holiday of autumn.

 Here's an important rule of the road, just about everywhere in the United States: ALL cars must STOP if a school bus is stopped with its red lights flashing. This means cars behind the bus AND cars coming in any other direction. (If the bus starts flashing yellow, slow down . . . it's about to stop!)

All cars must remain completely stopped until the bus turns off the flashing red lights. (We want those kids to be safe getting on and off the school bus!)

You remember that Memorial Day weekend in May is the unofficial start of summer. Well, Americans think of Labor Day weekend as the unofficial start of autumn. Labor Day is always celebrated on the first Monday of September, and you know what that means...Yes, three-day weekend! No school! No work! Labor Day celebrates workers, so what better way to celebrate than by a long weekend of NOT working? Ha! Families can enjoy one last, long weekend of cookouts. After the quiet of summer while people are on vacation, cities get busy again as people return to work. Hey, **commuters**! Welcome back to **rush hour**! Sorry about the traffic . . .

But going back to school isn't the only sign of fall. There's a **chill** in the air. The leaves are changing with beautiful displays of brilliant color. The air feels fresh, the days are cool, and the **crisp scent** of fallen leaves calls everyone outside. Ha—to **RAKE** those leaves! Here's a **picture-perfect** Saturday: Mom and Dad are working in the yard, raking all the leaves into **piles**. *Not* so perfect: the kids come running and jump in the piles! FUN! Fun for the kids, not so much fun for the parents who have to start raking **all over again**.

Are you **exhausted** from raking all those leaves? We have good news for you! Thanks to another autumn activity, you'll get to sleep an extra hour. YAY! The first Sunday in November is the day people in most of the country

CORN MAZE

turn their clocks back an hour. Think it's 2:00 a.m.? Not anymore! Change that clock so it says 1:00 a.m. This is the end of Daylight Saving Time. Bye-bye, nice, long, sunny summer days. Some people think, "spring forward, fall back" to remember how to change the clock. We just think, "An extra hour of sleep! Yay!" Ha, we all may need that extra sleep to get ready for the fall holidays . . .

Autumn is a great time for a day in the country. Lots of farms plan activities that are fun for the whole family, like corn **mazes** and **hayrides**. What's a corn maze, you ask? A farmer will cut a trail through his cornfield with lots of **dead-end** paths. Because corn plants grow so tall, they seem like a wall all along the paths. Think you've found the exit? Dead end! Go back and try another path. Have a race with the kiddies. See who can find their way out of the maze first. Hint: Bring a map! We hope you find the exit before dark—those **scarecrows** can be really **spooky** at night! Sure, their job is to **scare** the birds away from eating the corn, but at night they just might scare YOU! (*Okay, me . . . They scare ME! Get me OUT OF HERE!*)

 By the end of November, we are so tired of **pumpkin**-*everything* that we can't wait for winter to arrive with a new flavor! In October and November, we've had pumpkin pie, pumpkin bread, pumpkin coffee, pumpkin cookies, pumpkin soup, pumpkin ice cream, pumpkin. . . *AAAAARGHHHHHH!!!!!!* ◀ **Now listen to Audio Track 19**
(transcript on page 217)

If you're able to escape from this crazy maze, you might want to save some time to relax on a hayride. People **hop on** a wagon that the farmer has covered with hay. He **hooks it up** to his **tractor**, and everyone takes a ride through the farm. It may be a **bumpy** ride, so find a spot with plenty of hay for a nice soft seat! Did we say, "Relax"? As you bump your way through the farm, you'll notice signs of the fall harvest everywhere: pumpkins, scarecrows, and **bales** of hay.

A lot of people like to take road trips to the mountains and woods of the **country** during the fall. These tourists are sometimes called **leaf peepers**, and they travel to places like New England just to enjoy the beautiful **foliage**

 The New England states are famous for fall sightseeing as the leaves change color, but everyone has a favorite destination: Skyline Drive in the Blue Ridge Mountains; Aspen, Colorado; the Cascades in the Northwest; and (our personal favorite): the Catskill Mountains of New York. Go! See the beautiful scenery! Send us a postcard!
◀ **Now listen to Audio Track 20**
(transcript on page 218)

and scenery. And if they're not looking at the trees, they're pulling the branches! Lots of families have a tradition of going apple picking in autumn. At pick-your-own **orchards**, you can choose sweet, juicy apples right on the tree. Of course, the fun part is eating one or two right there in the field as you pick. YUM! It's so much fun to pick the apples that most people have way too many, but that's okay—you'll have plenty for those back-to-school **lunch boxes**. In a field full of pumpkins, let the kids pick a special one to **carve** into a **jack-o-lantern**. Don't forget the **apple cider**! Ooh, and those apple cider donuts . . . . Somebody STOP US!

Halloween and Thanksgiving are the **biggest** fall holidays for most Americans, but there are also religious holidays that some Americans observe. For example, many Hindu Americans celebrate Diwali, a joyous festival of lights. Jewish people celebrate Rosh Hashanah, the Jewish New Year, and Yom Kippur, a day of self-examinination and prayer. Muslim Americans celebrate Eid al-Adha with special prayers. These holidays may be in autumn, but the dates are determined by the lunar calendar, so they will change from year to year.

There are very important civic holidays that Americans observe in fall. We honor **veterans** on November 11. Veterans Day is for *all* people who have served in the military. (On Memorial Day, in May, we honor the people who have died while serving.) Many veterans get together for ceremonies to remember their service for the country that they love. They always begin by honoring the country and the flag. Many people show extra respect when they meet a veteran. Some people like to do something special, like pay for a veteran's coffee at a coffee shop. Once, my dad went through **security** at an airport. He had his military **medals** in his **carry-on bag**. The security **agent** asked him to wait just a minute. The man returned with his **supervisor**. The supervisor **shook hands** with my dad, and said, "Thank you for your service. I'm honored to meet a veteran of World War II." My dad was surprised and very **moved** by the man's kindness and respect. Veterans don't expect to be honored. They feel they were just serving their country. Veterans Day is a good time to remember how important these people are to our country's freedom.

And if you watch TV, I'm sure you know about the other civic holiday! Election Day is the Tuesday after the first Monday in November, and **candidates** are **driving everyone crazy** with too many **ads** on TV! "Vote for me!" "No, vote for ME!" "NO, vote for . . . " Well, you get the idea. Still, it's a very important day when citizens should carefully choose their leaders and vote. Some elections are for a national office, like **senator** or **representative to Congress**. Some are for a local town office, like mayor or **city council**. Usually there are important decisions to vote on, too. Maybe your town wants you to decide if money should go to schools or to other special projects. These are important **issues**, so people should go to the polls and **make their voices heard**. Sometimes people like to **complain** a lot about what politicians are doing; if people get off the **couch** and go vote, they can make their voices heard. **Vote them in**, or vote them out!

TAKE A LOOK: Commonly Confused Words

They sound very similar . . . They look kind of similar... But don't be tricked! There are lots of words in English that are very easily confused . . . even by native speakers. We're here to help you figure them out . . . and use them perfectly every time. Here are some common tricky pairs:

accept: receive/take something
*I'm happy to **accept** your gift!*

except: not including
*I like all my classes **except** Cooking. Haha!*

---

affect: cause a change
*One late train **affects** all the others after it.*

effect: a result or consequence
*One **effect** of the late train was that many people were late for work.*

---

capitol: important civic building
*The politicians have offices in the **capitol**.*

capital: city where the government is located
*The **capital** of the U.S. is Washington, D.C.*

---

conscience: feelings of right and wrong
*His **conscience** wouldn't let him tell a lie.*

conscious: awake; aware
*When visitors arrived after her surgery, she was **conscious**, but in a little pain.*

compliment: a nice thing to say about someone or something
*Thanks for the **compliment** about my new sweater!*

complement: something that makes another thing perfect or complete
*I think some fruit will be the perfect **complement** to my soup-and-salad lunch.*

---

personal: about someone
*He talked about learning English as a taxicab driver, and the students loved his funny **personal** stories.*

personnel: People who work in a place
*In the snow emergency, all office **personnel** were told to stay home. Yay, snow!*

---

precede: come before
*A short talk about the music will **precede** the concert.*

proceed: continue; go forward
*He kept the talk short so the concert could **proceed** on time.*

---

principal: leader of a school; an important person in an organization
*The **principal** greeted the students each morning.*
*As a **principal** in the company, he voted to raise cash by selling stock.*

principle: important thing
*The country was built on **principles** of freedom and justice for everyone.*

---

quiet: Shhhhh!!!
Quiet! The baby's sleeping!

quite: very
*In fact, the baby's been sleeping for **quite** a long time.*

---

stationary: not moving
Stationary exercise bikes are so weird! I pedal and pedal, but I don't go anywhere!

stationery: writing paper and writing supplies
*E-mail and texting are great, but I still love to write a letter on beautiful **stationery**.*

YOUR TURN!

Give it a try! Circle the commonly confused word that fits the sentence. Answers are on page 189.

1. Hey, Dad, we have a long weekend coming up. How about a road trip to the **capitol/capital** to see the White House?

2. Everyone's happy when the kids go back to school. Well, **accept/except** the kids, of course!

3. The prediction of perfect beach weather really **affected/effected** traffic—there were tons of cars on the road. *Aaaarghhhhh!!!!*

4. Parents usually think it's bad news to get a call from the **principal/principle** of their child's school . . . And they're usually right!

5. It might look tricky, but actually it's **quiet/quite** easy to carve a jack-o-lantern.

6. People remain **stationary/stationery** during the flag ceremony on Veterans Day.

7. A cup of apple cider is the perfect **compliment/complement** to a seasonal snack.

8. I'm glad I voted. I think the new leader has a strong **conscience/conscious** and will do only what is best for the community.

9. Are you going through the corn maze at night? Make sure to **precede/proceed** carefully—those scarecrows aren't **quiet/quite** as scary if you see them first!

10. The neighborhood kids loved Jim's fun **personal/personnel** style of pumpkin carving. His jack-o-lanterns always had crazy faces only he could create!

VOCABULARY

- **ad:** advertisement
- **agent:** a worker representing an organization
- ⓘ **all over again:** another time, from the beginning
- **apple cider:** drink made from apples. Try some at an orchard—yum!
- **back to school:** the time that unofficially marks the beginning of fall; when all the kiddies go to school again after the summer vacation.
- **bale:** a bundle of something gathered into a stack or pile

- ⓘ **biggest:** most popular
- **bumpy:** not smooth
- **candidate:** someone who wants to be elected to a government position
- **carry-on bag:** what you bring onto an airplane
- **carve:** cut with a sharp knife
- **chill:** feeling of coolness
- **city council:** a group of elected officials (working in local government)
- **commuter:** a person who travels back and forth to work every day
- **complain:** talk about how something is not good
- **couch:** sofa
- **country:** places where there are few cities—just farms, mountains, and woods
- **crisp:** weather that is fresh and cool
- **dead end:** a path that ends without connecting to another path. (When used as an adjective, it has a hyphen.)
- ⓘ **drive someone crazy:** annoy someone!
- **exhausted:** very, very, *very* tired!
- **foliage:** the leaves on trees and plants (turning beautiful colors in fall)
- **hayride:** a ride in a wagon filled with hay, pulled by a farm vehicle
- **hook (something) up:** connect something to something else
- ⓘ **hop on; hop in:** get onto or into a vehicle
- **issues:** important topics and ideas
- **jack-o-lantern:** pumpkin carved into a face
- ⓘ **leaf peepers:** people who like to travel to see areas with beautiful fall leaves
- **lunch box:** decorated box that kids (and adults!) use to bring their lunch to school (or work)
- **make your voice heard:** have an official take note of your opinion
- **maze:** a puzzle of paths that you go into and then try to find a way out
- **medals:** awards; often worn on shirts for military people, or on ribbons around the neck for sports
- **moved; to be moved:** to feel a strong emotion
- **orchard:** a group of fruit trees
- ⓘ **picture-perfect:** perfect! could not be better!
- **pile:** stack; group of things on top of each other
- **pumpkin:** that big orange fruit (yes, FRUIT!) that becomes ripe in fall
- **rake:** use a special tool (a rake!) to move leaves out of grass

- **representative to Congress:** elected official to the U.S. Senate or House of Representatives
- **rush hour:** morning and afternoon times when everybody is traveling to and from work. Traffic!
- **scare:** frighten
- **scarecrows:** figures made of sticks and cloth to scare birds away from planted fields
- **scent:** a nice smell
- **security:** feeling that everything is safe; at the airport, where passengers and bags are checked
- **senator:** elected official to the legislative body in federal or state government
- **shake hands** (past tense: shook)**:** a common greeting and sign of respect
- **sharpen:** make a pencil have a point; also, make something (like a photo) clearer
- ⓘ **smiling from ear to ear:** very, very happy! (That's a *big* smile!)
- ⓘ **spooky:** scary! frightening
- **supervisor:** boss for a group of workers
- **three Rs:** Not really! But they sound like they begin with *r*: **R**eading, w**R**iting, and a**R**ithmetic
- **tractor:** a large farm vehicle
- **veteran:** someone who has served in the armed services (military)
- **vote them in/out:** If you're happy with an official's work on important issues, vote for him or her; otherwise, vote for the *other* candidate to take his job!

COLUMBUS DAY

In fourteen hundred ninety-two (1492)
Columbus sailed the ocean blue.

Yes, around the second Monday of every October, little kids across America are sitting at their little desks, **proud** to **recite** that little poem about the **discovery** of America by Christopher Columbus. Do YOU want to tell those cute little kids they're wrong? We sure don't! Here's the traditional story that generations of Americans learned:

Christopher Columbus was an Italian **explorer** in the 1400s. People in Europe around this time wanted spices, **perfume**, and **silk** from Asia, but it was very hard to travel there by land. Columbus had a **genius** idea! He thought he knew a **shortcut** to Asia and the Indies that would make **trade** much easier for Europeans.

Writing numbers can be tricky!

When we talk about **centuries** (time periods of 100 years), we usually say and spell the numbers like this:

- the 1400s
- the fourteen-hundreds

For **decades** (tens of years), we say and spell:

- the seventies
- the nineties

For decades *with* the century, we write the number, with an "s" to make it plural, and we say:

- the 1970s
- the nineteen seventies

And, to say a specific year, we say:

- twenty eighteen [2018]
- fourteen ninety-two [1492]

(*Aaaaackkk!!!* DO NOT add an apostrophe! Adding apostrophes for plurals is our **pet peeve**!)

Columbus got **financing** from the Queen of Spain, and he **set sail** with three ships: the *Niña*, the *Pinta*, and the *Santa María*. His "shortcut" was a **route** sailing west instead of east. (Okay, class, are you still with us?) It was **actually** a pretty good idea, except for one little problem: There's a **continent** between Europe and the Indies! This is a good time to **take a look** at a map:

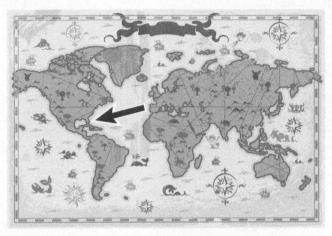

 Speaking of maps . . . Of course, you remember the seven continents! In English they are: North **A**merica, South **A**merica, Europe, **A**frica, **A**sia, **A**ustralia, and **A**ntarctica. HEY! Did you notice that they all start with "A" except *Europe*? Hmmm...

Anyway . . . . Columbus sailed west to get to Asia and the Indies, but he arrived at the islands of the Caribbean instead. It was a big surprise that this was a "New World"; but Columbus was looking for the Indies, so he called the people he met "Indians." And here's an interesting little **fact** that a lot of Americans don't know: Columbus never **set foot on** the land that's now America!

Anyway . . . Even if Columbus *did* set foot in America, **guess what**! There were people **already** there! The Native Americans were already living in America! (Besides, everyone is pretty sure the Vikings from Scandinavia **beat** Columbus in "discovering" America, but that's another story. ☺)

Anyway . . . Today, Columbus Day is celebrated on the second Monday in October. It's a public holiday, but not every state **observes** it. Some schools are open, but some may close for the holiday. Many government offices are closed, but many businesses are open. Look for big Columbus Day sales in stores. (We don't know why it's special to buy a **toaster** on Columbus Day—maybe to "discover" toast? Haha!—but we like **sales** for any reason! Hey! Maybe we have *sales* because Columbus had **sails**! Ha! Yay, Columbus!)

In many places Columbus Day has become a celebration of Italian American culture. (Okay, the Queen of *Spain* paid for his little vacation **cruise**, but remember that Columbus was *Italian*!) In New York City more than half a million people watch the Columbus Day Parade along Fifth Avenue! That's what we call a big Italian American celebration!

 Not everyone thinks Columbus is a person to celebrate. There is another **perspective** about him. Some people think that soon after Columbus arrived, he and the nations of Europe began to **exploit** the **native** peoples and **destroy** their culture. It's a controversial holiday for many people in the U.S. In fact, some places use this day to show the importance of celebrating and respecting native peoples and cultures.

TAKE A LOOK: More Commonly Confused Words

Are you ready? Here are some more of our pet peeves! These words sound *exactly* the same, and lots of people aren't careful about writing the correct one. But we know *you'll* be careful! (We just love making you smarter!)

THERE/THEY'RE/THEIR

There

1. a place
   - Your book is over **there**, on the table.
   - That concert was great! I'm so glad I was **there**.
2. used in the expressions *there is* and *there are* to show that something exists. (We often use *there's*, the contracted form for *there is*, but we *don't* usually shorten *there are*.)
   - **There is** a new coffee shop in the neighborhood.
   - **There's** a new donut shop, too! Decisions, decisions—where should we go first?
   - **There are** coffee shops and donut shops . . . it's the perfect neighborhood!

They're

—the contracted (short) form of *they are*

- Our new neighbors are from England. ***They're*** such nice people, and we love to hear that British accent!
- ***They're*** coming with us to the new coffee shop.

Their

—the possessive adjective meaning *belonging to them*

- ***Their*** kids are best friends with our kids, so we spend lots of time together.
- I'm not sure ***their*** mom likes it, but the kids are losing ***their*** British accent already!

TOO, TO, TWO

too

1. shows an excess of something
   - It's ***too*** hot! I don't like playing tennis in this high heat.
   - Wow, I can't buy that new device—it's ***too*** expensive!
2. *also*, or *in addition*
   - We admit it—we love coffee, but we like tea, ***too***.
   - Although he studies English now, he wants to learn Italian, ***too***.

to

1. a preposition showing *where*
   - I drive ***to*** the office every day.
   - Hey, that donut looks yummy! I'll take an extra one and give it ***to*** my pal.
2. shows the infinitive form of a verb
   - It's a lucky thing I like ***to drive***!
   - And, okay, we'll admit it—we love ***to eat***!

two

—the number after *one*!

- Yes, please. I would like ***two*** donuts!
- After all, I have ***two*** hands—one for each donut!

ITS/IT'S

its

—possessive adjective meaning belonging *to it.* (no apostrophe!)

- The pooch wagged *its* tail like crazy! It was happy to see us come home.
- My cell phone has *its* own special case.

It's

1. the contracted (short) form of *it is.* (yes apostrophe!)
   - These cookies are so delicious *it's* impossible to eat only one!
   - *It's* a good thing I have two hands!

2. the contracted (short) form of *it has*, when used in those complicated verb tenses you just love! You know the ones we mean—those tenses that show something started in the past, and continued (or *is continuing*!) up to the present. (Think: *present perfect* or *present perfect continuous. Aaaackkkk!*)
   - *It's* taken all week to finish this report! (*It has taken* = present perfect)
   - *It's* been so cold this week! (*It has* been = present perfect)
   - *It's* been snowing for two days. (*It has been snowing* = present perfect continuous)
   - My laptop is old. *It's* been taking a long time to open files. (*It has been taking* = present perfect continuous)

YOUR TURN!

How careful can *you* be? Choose the correct answer. Answers are on page 189.

1. Mom, look over **there/their/they're! It's/Its** a giant scarecrow!

2. The neighbors are taking **there/they're/their** three kids and our **too/to/two** children for a hayride.

3. But no one wants to try the corn maze at night—it's **too/to/two** scary!

4. Hey, if we get **there/their/they're** early enough, maybe we'll have time for apple picking, **too/to/two**.

5. I think **its/it's** going to be cold, so be sure the kids bring **there/their/they're** coats.

6. **There are/Their are/They're** Columbus Day parades in lots of big cities.

7. It's important **too/to/two** respect our veterans for **there/their/they're** service to the country.

8. **There/Their/They're** leaving work early so they have time **to/two/too** vote.

9. Columbus thought he had a great idea for travel **to/two/too** the Indies. Queen Isabella of Spain thought so, **to/two/too**.

10. The kids are back in school, so **its/it's** important to drive carefully.

☑ FALL HOLIDAYS INFO TO KNOW:

☑ First let's talk about what you should *not* do! Many people have very strong opinions about political subjects and politicians. Especially around election time, people may like to express these opinions—and not always in a respectful way. Just look at social media! Be careful at parties or among friends! Of course, it's fine to disagree with someone's opinion, but in a polite way. If people get angry, it's probably best just to **change the subject**. Some people say, "Never talk about politics at a party!"

☑ Go to a parade! Watch the **marching bands**! Eat some Italian treats like **gelato** and **cannoli!** (*ooh*—cannoli! Save one for us!)

☑ Go shopping! Look in your local newspaper for ads. There will be sales at malls everywhere. "BACK-TO-SCHOOL SAVINGS!" "VETERANS DAY SPECIAL!" "COLUMBUS DAY SALE!" Well, you get the idea . . .

☑ Call some friends and plan a trip to a local farm for a hayride. Or challenge your friends to survive a haunted corn maze! While everyone tries to find a path out of the field, actors dressed as monsters or horror movie characters will jump out and try to scare everyone. **Only the strong survive!**

✓ Be sensitive to what may be offensive to other people. Cultural and ethnic groups often have preferences about how they wish to be identified. For example, when Americans talk about the people who lived here before explorers from other places "discovered" it, we call the people "Native Americans." Many people of this native ancestry think it's rude when others call them "Indians."

 There's a lot of **controversy** in the United States about some sports teams with Native American names, like the Cleveland Indians, the Washington Redskins, and the Atlanta Braves. Some people feel that the Native American symbols they use are disrespectful of their culture. They feel that the names and symbols **make fun of** Native American heritage.

Other people think that the teams are showing respect for Native American culture. They say that the symbols represent the good, strong qualities of the teams.

What do you think? Would you like to have a sports team represent your culture with a funny symbol?

YOUR TURN!

Write T (True) or F (False) for these Columbus Day statements. Answers are on page 189.

1. _____ Columbus was sent by Italy to find a new route to the Indies.

2. _____ Children learn that Columbus sailed with only one ship.

3. _____ Columbus arrived in "the New World" in 1492.

4. _____ Christopher Columbus landed in Washington, D.C., and said, "Wow, this must be America!"

5. _____ The Viking explorers from Scandinavia were probably in North America before Columbus.

6. _____ Everyone believes that Columbus and other explorers respected the culture of the native people they met.

7. _____ Today, parades celebrate Italian American culture on Columbus Day.

8. _____ Columbus Day is celebrated on the second Tuesday in October.

9. _____ All businesses are closed on Columbus Day.

10. _____ Your favorite authors love Italian cannoli. (Don't get this one wrong!)

FUN WITH IDIOMATIC EXPRESSIONS: Sailing Along!

- **sail right through something:** do something very easily
  *She was really nervous about the English test, but it was so easy she **sailed right through it**.*

- **completely at sea:** very confused
  *He had never been on the New York City subway before, so he was **completely at sea** when he tried to find the right train at the busy station!*

- **knock the wind out of someone's sails:** make someone lose confidence in something he was proud of
  *Aki was so proud that he won the race, until officials **knocked the wind out of his sails** by announcing that a technical error disqualified him.*

- **shipshape:** neat and clean
  *Trouble in the college dorm! James likes the room **shipshape**, but his roommate is very messy. Uh-oh!*

- **clear sailing:** easy to do, with no problems
  *Getting all the applications and documents prepared was stressful but once that was done, it was **clear sailing** planning the college visit.*

 JUST FOR FUN!

 In many cities, public officials and **celebrities** invite people to "be Italian for a day!" There may be **street fairs** where vendors will sell special Italian foods and **desserts**. Italian cheesecake . . . cannoli . . . gelato . . . And PIZZA! Oh boy, somebody stop us!

 Big cities that have large ethnic populations often have neighborhoods where large groups of Italian American people live. New York City, Chicago, Baltimore, San Francisco, and lots of other American cities have neighborhoods called "Little Italy." These are the places to go if you want to experience customs and **authentic** foods. There are lots of cafés and restaurants, and in places like the Italian Market neighborhood of Philadelphia, you'll find street after street of ethnic shops and outdoor vendors. *Ciao!*

VOCABULARY

- **actually:** really; in fact
- **already:** before now, or before the time mentioned
- ⓘ **anyway . . . :** an expression that brings you back to the main topic after talking about something else
- **authentic:** real, actual
- **beat:** do something before (or better than) someone else
- **cannoli:** *mmmm….* Italian treats made of crisp, flat wafers rolled around cream. (Hey, save some for us!)
- **celebrity:** famous person
- **century:** 100 years
- **change the subject:** talk about something else
- **continent:** one of the seven largest areas of land on the Earth
- **controversy:** an issue that many people strongly disagree about
- **cruise:** a voyage by boat, often for fun and vacation
- **decade:** ten years
- **dessert:** the BEST part of a meal—the sweets after all the food!
- **destroy:** ruin; damage completely
- **discovery:** finding something new
- **exploit:** to use for your own good, even if it harms others
- **explorer:** someone who likes traveling and looking for new things
- **fact:** something that is true
- **financing:** a lot of money for a big project
- **gelato:** very creamy Italian ice cream
- **genius:** someone who is SUPER intelligent!
- ⓘ **guess what!:** an expression that shows excitement about what you are going to say next
- **make fun of:** laugh about something others think is very serious
- **marching bands:** organized groups of people playing loud music, usually in a parade
- **native:** person or thing that was always in a place
- **observe:** celebrate an occasion; also, to see
- ⓘ **only the strong survive:** a funny way to say an activity is really hard or challenging
- **perfume:** that fancy liquid containing nice-smelling oils
- **perspective:** view; opinion
- **pet peeve:** something that someone else finds really, *really* annoying

- **proud:** feeling good about something
- **recite:** to repeat from memory
- **route:** the way or path to get somewhere
- **sails:** large pieces of material on a boat to catch the wind for movement
- **sales:** special low prices offered by stores
- **set foot on:** walk on (something or someplace) for the first time
- **set sail:** start on a voyage by ship
- **shortcut:** an easier way to do something or go somewhere
- **silk:** delicate and expensive cloth, made from soft fibers produced by silkworms
- **street fair:** celebration with food and activities in a street that is closed to traffic for the occasion
- **survive:** live through a difficult situation
- ⓘ **take a look:** look at carefully
- **toaster:** the appliance that makes the toast!
- **trade:** business; buying and selling

"TRICK OR TREAT!"

That can only mean one thing: It's Halloween! This holiday on October 31 is a favorite for kids . . . and lots of grown-ups, too. On Halloween night, **witches**, **ghosts**, and **monsters** parade through the neighborhood with princesses, **superheroes** and **cartoon characters**. They ring doorbells and shout, "Trick or treat!" The neighbor will open her door and give candy to each kid. Wow! Free candy! Kids also know to respect the **code** of **trick-or-treating**: if a neighbor's lights are off, kids should not stop at that house. Maybe that neighbor doesn't like to celebrate Halloween. Or maybe she has **run out of** candy!

Kids also learn that it's important to be safe. Trick-or-treaters usually go in groups of friends (it's more fun!), and with an adult to make sure they're safe.

You may hear little Charlotte next door asking her mom, "Awww, Mom, can't I just go by myself with my friends?" **I bet** her mom will answer, "Not yet. Maybe when you're a little older." It's also a good idea for kids to carry a

The words are *trick or treat*. In kid language they mean "Please give us candy, or we will play a trick on you." (The kids don't really play tricks—if you don't have a treat, they just go to the next house!)

So when that doorbell rings, and little ghosts and monsters are hoping for candy, what you will hear is "TRICKATREAT!" It sounds like one (very excited!) word.

◀ **Now listen to Audio Track 21**
(transcript above and on page 219)

flashlight so people can see them. Adults need to be careful driving around on Halloween—the kids are very excited, and they may be running across the streets without looking for cars. Watch out, Charlotte!

Have you seen these cute little triangles? Do they look like vegetables to you? Haha! Not even close! They're sugar, sugar, sugar! We wonder if anyone is fooled by their almost-vegetable name—candy CORN. It's a really popular treat around Halloween, but NOT for trick-or-treaters.

Most parents allow kids to eat only the candy that is wrapped. Candy corn and other unwrapped treats may not be safe to eat.

Enjoy this not-a-vegetable at home, but don't give it to trick-or-treaters!

Halloween is a pretty big holiday in the U.S., but not everyone celebrates it. Some people don't like Halloween for religious reasons. Some people don't like the idea of ghosts and witches. These families may choose to do other fall activities that celebrate the harvest, like picking apples.

Although not everyone likes Halloween, there are lots of adults who enjoy **getting into the spirit of** things. They have costume parties for their friends. They may decorate their houses to make them look **scary**. Some adults even like to dress up in costumes to surprise the trick-or-treaters. Haha, kids—BOO! Teenagers (and adults!) like to visit **haunted houses** where they walk through a dark and scary building. These haunted houses may have actors dressed up in scary costumes to **frighten** people. *Noooo!* Not us! We don't like to be scared! Just give us the candy!

TAKE A LOOK: Even More Commonly Confused Words

Yes, we have even *more* pet peeves! Does that mean we're cranky? Noooooo! We just like making tricky English stuff easier . . .

YOUR/YOU'RE

your

—possessive adjective meaning *belonging to you*

- *Your* teacher is excited!
- She can see that all the practice is helping *your* English pronunciation.

you're

—the contracted (short) form of *you are*

- *You're* such a great student! Keep practicing!
- If *you're* ever in our city, please come visit us.

BY/BYE/BUY

by

—near

- The donut shop is *by* the coffee shop.
- Too bad it's not *by* the gym. Haha!

bye

—good-bye

- *Bye*! I'll see you tomorrow.
- *Bye*!!!

buy

—purchase

- I really need to *buy* a new car.
- I also need to *buy* some donuts!! (Okay, maybe I don't need to, but I sure do want to!)

ARE/OUR

are

—form of the verb *to be*

- We *are* going to Hawaii on vacation, lucky us!
- You *are* so sweet to bring me coffee and donuts for breakfast!

our

—possessive adjective meaning *belonging to us*

- Yes, Hawaii is *our* dream vacation!
- Let's leave *our* kids with Grandma when we go! (Thanks, Grandma!)

YOUR TURN!

Are you ready for *our* little quiz on even more commonly confused words? Choose the correct answer. Answers are on page 190.

1. **Are/Our** kids can't wait to go trick-or-treating! **By/Bye/Buy**, kids! Have fun!

2. We see lots of kids in **are/our** new neighborhood. I think I may need to **by/bye/buy** more Halloween treats.

3. Haha! **Your/You're** planning to dress as a monster this Halloween! Aren't you worried that you may scare **your/you're** kids?

4. Oh boy, we need to **by/bye/buy** new costumes for **are/our** kids this year. They've grown so much!

5. It was fun to see **your/you're** kids last night. They were so cute with their little pumpkins!

6. I love **your/you're** Halloween decorations! Did you **by/bye/buy** the scarecrow at **are/our** local farm?

7. We **are/our** always happy to hear the trick-or-treaters say, "Thank you!"

8. Wow—look at the crazy spider web **by/bye/buy** the front door! No thanks—I think I'll skip that house!

✅ HALLOWEEN INFO TO KNOW:

Parents usually take their children trick-or-treating. When the kids are older, they go with friends. Even if you would like to be friendly, do NOT invite children into the house. If you don't have your candy near the door, the kids will wait.

Kids like to get compliments on their costumes. "Wow, what a scary monster!" Or "You look just like a princess!" We always say, "Have fun, kids!"

Some Halloween parties have a special activity called ***bobbing*** *for apples*. There is a large tub of water filled with floating apples. You try to get an apple using only your teeth—no hands allowed! Some of the apples may have a special coin inside. Don't forget a towel!

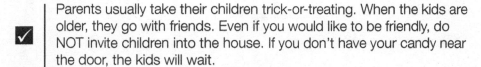

Have you heard the saying "An apple a day keeps the doctor away"? Farm-fresh fruit is a healthy snack for everyone, so eat lots of apples. (Haha! But if the apples are in *pies* when you eat them, they may not be quite so healthy!)

Speaking of pie… we have another expression: "as American as apple pie." Like baseball, the all-American sport, apple pie is a symbol of something being typically American.

Eat apples! Eat pie! Then play baseball to exercise and burn those calories!

Making **candy apples** is another (delicious!) Halloween activity. These are apples on a stick, covered with a red hard candy or yummy caramel. Some farms will show you how to make them, or you can just buy some. Don't tell your dentist!

Go with friends (and the kids!) to a **pumpkin patch** and choose a big pumpkin to carve into a jack-o-lantern. Scary? Funny? Have a contest and see who has the best design! Then rinse the seeds, sprinkle with salt, and roast them in the oven for a fun snack. Yum!

YOUR TURN

Do you recognize the scary pictures below? They're all signs of Halloween. Try to match the words to the pictures. Answers are on page 190.

1. _____ witch's broom
2. _____ Halloween candy
3. _____ ghost
4. _____ jack-o-lantern
5. _____ haunted house
6. _____ black cat
7. _____ bats
8. _____ witch's hat
9. _____ candle
10. _____ skull
11. _____ tombstone
12. _____ witch's cauldron

FUN WITH IDIOMATIC EXPRESSIONS: Ghosts and Skeletons!

- **Give up the ghost:** stop working completely
  *Bad news! I need to buy a new car; my old one finally **gave up the ghost**.*

- **ghost town:** a town that has no one living there; describes a place that used to have people, but there's no one there now.
  *The worker went into the office over the Christmas holidays, but it was like a **ghost town**!*

 Ghost towns can be fun tourist attractions, or they may be places that you hope never to see. In the West and Southwest, there are towns that were very busy in the **Wild West** days of **cowboys** and mining. It's fun to imagine the excitement of people looking for gold and hoping to become rich.

But there are also towns where people used to live that are mostly abandoned... and NOT exciting. In New York State, there's a town near Niagara Falls called Love Canal. People used to live there as in any other town. But then people became very sick. Many people developed cancer, and children were born with very serious problems. Finally, scientists found that a company had **dumped** toxic (deadly) **chemical waste** that was **polluting** the town.

The government has cleaned up the toxic chemicals, and some people live in nearby neighborhoods, but Love Canal is a ghost town that's too scary for us—we'll take the Wild Wild West!

- **Not a ghost of a chance:** No chance at all!
  Five-year-old boy: Mom, can I have an iPhone?
  *Mom: **Not a ghost of a chance!***

- **skeleton in the closet:** a big, bad, embarrassing secret that someone is hiding
  *The politician hoped no one would discover the **skeleton in his closet**: He hadn't paid his taxes for five years.*

- **skeleton crew:** the smallest number of workers possible to keep a business open
  *So many workers want time off for Christmas that the company stays open with a **skeleton crew**.*

JUST FOR FUN!

How to Carve a Jack-O-Lantern

1. Find a really big pumpkin at the supermarket, farmer's market, or pumpkin patch.
2. Cover a table with plastic bags or old newspapers. You'll be glad you did—this is going to be **messy**!

3. Think of a crazy, fun, or scary (but **simple**!) design for Mr. O'Lantern. (You can find designs online or at the store.) Draw the design on the pumpkin.
4. Using a sharp knife, cut a large piece from the top.
5. Here's the fun part: put your hand inside and pull out all the gooey seeds and stuff. *Eeew!*
6. When the inside is nice and clean, cut out your design.
7. Put a candle inside.
8. Put it outside your door, and scare all the kids away! (More candy for you! Haha!) Happy Halloween!

VOCABULARY

- **bobbing:** going up and down in water
- **candy apple:** an apple on a stick, covered with caramel or red hard candy (Because. . . why not?!)
- **cartoon character:** an animated person or creature drawn as a picture
- **chemical waste:** poisonous stuff left after making certain products
- **code:** rules that people follow in a situation
- **cowboys:** men on horses who take care of cows; usually in the western states of the United States
- **dump:** throw away without care; dispose of trash or water
- **flashlight:** small light that you carry
- **frighten:** scare; make someone afraid
- **get into the spirit (of something):** to show that you enjoy an activity; doing a fun thing
- **ghosts:** spirits that are invisible (unseen); they make scary noises!

- **haunted house:** a place decorated to be scary and fun for Halloween
- ⓘ **I bet:** shows that I think something is true
- **messy:** not neat and orderly; not clean
- **monster:** large, scary creature
- **polluting:** making dirty and unsafe
- **pumpkin patch:** an area of pumpkins growing on a farm
- **run out of (something):** to have no more of something left. We run out of candy on Halloween because we eat so much of it before the kids arrive!
- **scary:** frightening
- **simple:** easy; plain
- **superhero:** a pretend character with special powers (like the ability to fly)
- **trick-or-treating:** going from house to house in a neighborhood to ask for candy on Halloween
- **Wild West:** the western states of the United States when they were first being settled, with many cowboys, many bad guys, and no laws!
- **witch:** scary woman character dressed in black who flies on a broom

THANKSGIVING

Are you hungry? Just thinking about Thanksgiving makes us hungry! Thanksgiving is one holiday where almost everyone enjoys a feast of fabulous foods . . . and almost everyone eats the same thing—turkey! In fact, many people call the holiday "Turkey Day"! It's a huge holiday that almost everyone celebrates, all across the country. But Thanksgiving is about much more than food. Celebrated on the fourth Thursday in November, this national holiday is all about getting together with family and friends. It's a day to remember and be *thankful* for all the good things that we have in life. Some people choose to add a religious prayer of thanks to their celebration, but almost everyone sees Thanksgiving as a day to think about and **appreciate** the important things: family, friends, food, and even the small things that **enrich** our lives.

Of course, there's a story that goes with the holiday! Have you been out shopping around Thanksgiving? You've probably seen pictures of those Pilgrim characters with the **tall** hats and the funny black and white clothes. You've probably seen Native American characters, too. And we *know* you've seen turkeys, and corn, and pumpkins!

Here's the traditional story of the first Thanksgiving:

Before our country became the United States, people called Pilgrims traveled here from England. They wanted to live where they would be free to practice the religion of their choice. The first Pilgrims sailed here on a ship called the *Mayflower*. It was a long **voyage**, and they arrived in what is now Massachusetts during a very cold winter. Many of the Pilgrims died because they couldn't find food. But the Native Americans who lived here showed the Pilgrims how to plant **crops** that would grow. In the fall they had a very **successful** harvest. They had food! The Native Americans had helped the Pilgrims to survive! They all celebrated with a huge feast.

Today, Thanksgiving is important to just about every American family. Millions of people watch big Thanksgiving Day parades to see floats with giant balloons of turkeys and cartoon characters. Airports and train stations are **chaotic** with crowds of people hurrying home to join their families for their own Thanksgiving feast. The menu is traditional: turkey with **stuffing**, **cranberry sauce**, **mashed potatoes**, **gravy**, baked **yams**, **squash**, green bean **casserole**, apple pie, pumpkin pie, **pecan** pie... YUM! I can't wait to **dig in**! But there's another modern tradition that goes along with the pumpkin pie: football! Yes, when you're so **stuffed** that you can't eat another thing, it's time to relax on the couch and cheer on your favorite American football team. Yes, it's Thanksgiving—family, friends, food, football, and . . . fun!

Are you still awake? Did you have a nice nap after your big meal? Then get ready for BLACK FRIDAY!

People like to joke about taking a nap after a big Thanksgiving dinner. They blame it on **tryptophan**, a science-y word about science-y stuff in the turkey. We're pretty sure feeling sleepy is more about the piles of food we just ate than the science-y stuff. . .

◀ **Now listen to Audio Track 22**
(transcript on page 219)

Although Black Friday is a traditional shopping day at malls, online shopping is so popular that lots of people just look for the best deals on the Internet, with their mobile device apps. Thanks to mobile devices, people can shop **24/7**, and there's no need to fight the crowds.

Some people love to plan this shopping adventure . . . and walking around the mall helps burn off some of the Thanksgiving dinner calories. Haha!

No thanks. Not us. Sign us up for online shopping in our pajamas on the sofa!

Yes, because Thanksgiving is always on a Thursday, many companies give their workers a holiday on Friday so they can have a long weekend. BEWARE! This is traditionally a HUGE shopping day! Some people look at their calendars and think, "Uh-oh! The next big holiday is almost here . . . It's time for Christmas shopping!" It is such a busy shopping day that it has a nickname: Black Friday. So many people spend this day buying things that some stores are **in the black** for the first time all year. Stores **compete** to **attract** shoppers with crazy **doorbusters** and sales. Each year, stores open earlier and earlier to get more and more shoppers—even in the middle of the night! Some places even open on Thanksgiving Day. Be prepared to **fight the crowds**—the malls will be **wall-to-wall** people on Black Friday. Don't say we didn't warn you!

Here's another controversial issue! There is some **backlash** to stores opening on Thanksgiving Day. Many people think the holiday should be one special day for families to spend time together, without thinking about shopping. And people who work in the stores have to leave their families to go to work.

What do you think? Should people be able to shop, shop, shop, even on big holidays? Or should there be some days when families just spend the day together?

◀ **Now listen to Audio Track 23**
(transcript on page 220)

TAKE A (LONG) LOOK: Using the word *long*

Everyone loves a long weekend, but no one likes a long day! Thanksgiving Day begins a long weekend that lots of people spend shopping. Other holidays mean long weekends in the mountains or at the beach, or just relaxing at home. Let's take a *long* look at how we use the word *long*.

- **long weekend:** a holiday is celebrated on Friday or Monday, adding a bonus no-work day to the Saturday and Sunday weekend. This is good!
- **long day:** the coffee machine at work is broken, you forgot your lunch, and the Internet is down. It's going to be a long day. This is bad!
- **long week:** It seems like things at work or school are not fun or easy, and the weekend seems far away. This is very bad!
- **so long:** good-bye
- **take a long look:** think about something in a very careful way.
- **long face:** a sad expression
- **long for:** want something (or someone!) very much
- **long shot:** something that is not very likely to happen
- **in the long run:** in the future; the end result of a situation
- **for the long haul:** for an extended period of time
- **go a long way:** be really helpful for something
- **has come a long way:** has made a lot of progress
- **make a long story short:** leave out unimportant information so the explanation is shorter. . .

YOUR TURN!

This won't take, um, *long*! Write one of the expressions from the list above that fits the sentences below. Answers are on page 191.

1. When he came to this country he didn't know one word of English. Now he's reading this book! He has _____.

2. Dad keeps buying lottery tickets. He knows it's a(n) _____, but he keeps hoping he'll win a million dollars. Good luck, Dad.

3. I'm hosting our Thanksgiving feast, but the oven isn't working, I lost my favorite stuffing recipe, there are problems at work, and it's only Monday! Oh yeah, it's going to be a(n) _____.

4. Hey, are you going home now? _____. See you tomorrow.

5. When he asked her to marry him, she knew that he would stay in the relationship _____.

6. All the preparations for the big Thanksgiving dinner are making me _____ my family far away.

7. I had absolutely no idea how to cook a turkey, but the pictures on the cooking website went _____ toward helping me make a perfect dinner!

8. I did it! I bought an electric car! It cost more to buy, but I think the money I'll save on gas will make it worth the expense _____.

9. Hey, why the _____? Your best friend will only be gone for a few weeks.

10. It's only one extra day, but I think everyone gets excited for a _____!

11. Oh no! The alarm didn't go off, I missed the bus, and I just noticed that I'm wearing two different shoes! It's going to be a(n) _____ _____.

12. It's a good idea to _____ at all the rules before you decide to move into a new apartment.

☑ THANKSGIVING INFO TO KNOW:

☑ Go to the Thanksgiving Parade! (Wear warm clothes.) Look for giant turkeys the size of a building! Or just sit on the couch at home . . . where it's nice and warm . . . watch the parade on TV . . . and have another piece of pie! (We know where we'll be!)

☑ If you're invited to share Thanksgiving dinner with a friend, ask if there's something you can bring. A special food from your country is a great idea! Flowers also make a nice hostess gift. It's polite to offer to help, both before and after the dinner. Ask, "What can I do?" "Is there anything I can do to help?" "Can I help you clean up?"

✓ If you're driving to someone's house, take some advice from us: Leave early! Sometimes roads and highways can seem more like parking lots on Thanksgiving. One little five-year-old we know got so hungry one very, very slow traffic Thanksgiving Day that he opened the box of pecan pie and started eating! Dig in, James!

✓ If you like adventure, go shopping on Black Friday. Only the strong survive! Some people make Black Friday shopping a tradition, and they plan their strategy to get the best deals! It's fun to get great prices on cool stuff, and if it gets too crazy, you can always try to find a seat for **people watching**!

YOUR TURN!

Can you complete the sentences with the best word? Answers are on page 191.

1. People came from England for religious freedom. They were called _____.

2. Like Columbus, these people _____ on ships to cross the Atlantic Ocean.

3. The new settlers had many problems until the _____ helped them survive.

4. The people learned what _____ would grow successfully.

5. The most important part of Thanksgiving is to _____ the good things we have.

6. One food that almost everyone eats on Thanksgiving is _____. Gobble, gobble!

7. Lots of people enjoy seeing the _____ in the Thanksgiving Parade.

8. The day after Thanksgiving is called _____.

9. Most stores have crazy _____ and sales so shoppers will come.

10. You won't find us at the mall with all those crazy shoppers. We'll be home, on the sofa, taking a nice _____. Haha!

FUN WITH IDIOMATIC EXPRESSIONS: Eating!

- **eat like a bird:** have a small appetite; eat very little
  *Our tiny Granny loves Thanksgiving and she cooks a huge meal for the family. Everyone else digs in, but not Granny—**she eats like a bird**.*

- **eat someone out of house and home:** have a big appetite; eat a lot of the food in the house!
  *Every time James comes home from college he **eats us out of house and home**! "Hey, Mom! When are you going to the supermarket?" (Answer: "I just went an hour ago!")*

- **my eyes are bigger than my stomach:** I took too much food!
  *It happens every Thanksgiving: I think I can eat it all, but **my eyes are bigger than my stomach**, and I can't finish my food.*

- **pig out:** eat too much of a favorite food
  *It only comes once a year, so I always **pig out** on pecan pie at Thanksgiving!*

- **have a lot on your plate:** be busy with too many stressful responsibilities
  *She's working full-time, taking care of her sick grandmother, and trying to take English classes. She really **has a lot on her plate** right now.*

JUST FOR FUN!

Would you like to have a pretty, traditional Thanksgiving decoration in your house? Try this!

1. Buy some apples, small vegetables, tiny pumpkins, or dried corn (sometimes called Indian corn) at the supermarket, farmer's market, or a local farm.

2. Find some nicely colored leaves at a park or in your yard. (Maple and oak trees have really pretty fall leaves.)

3. Use a large clear or white bowl. Put some leaves in the bottom and around the sides, and then arrange the other items in the bowl. Add more leaves around the apples, corn, and pumpkins.

4. Tie a pretty gold and brown colored ribbon into a bow. (A flower pattern would be perfect!) Put the bow on top. You can let extra ribbon hang down the outside of the bowl. Voilà! (Yes, we know that's French. . . but we say it, too!)

5. Add cloves and other nice-smelling spices for a beautiful fall scent! Can we come see it?

VOCABULARY

- ⓘ **24/7:** 24 hours a day, 7 days a week = every minute of the day!
- **appreciate:** be thankful for something
- **attract:** get the attention of (someone)
- **backlash:** very strong, negative reaction to something
- **casserole:** a dish prepared from many ingredients, such as meat, vegetables, and rice. *Mmmmm!*
- **chaotic:** so busy there is no order; very confusing
- **compete:** try to do something better than someone else
- **cranberry sauce:** a jelly prepared from cranberries. It's great with turkey!
- **crops:** the plants that are grown on a farm
- ⓘ **dig in:** eat with enthusiasm
- ⓘ **doorbuster:** a special sale with very, very, very low prices on an expensive item so lots of shoppers will come to the store

- **enrich:** make better
- ⓘ **fight the crowds:** try to move around in a very crowded area
- **gravy:** brown sauce made from meat juices…totally awesome!
- **in the black:** making a profit ("in the red" is to be losing money)
- **mashed potatoes:** potatoes that are whipped with milk and butter. YUM!
- **pecan:** a delicious nut that grows in the southern parts of the United States
- **people watching:** sitting in a public place just watching people (because it's fun!)
- **squash:** a fall vegetable
- **stuffed:** the feeling of having eaten too much food
- **stuffing:** a special dish of bread pieces and seasonings cooked inside a turkey (our favorite!)
- **successful:** worked well
- **tall:** high
- **tryptophan:** a chemical compund in turkey that some people say causes sleepiness
- **voyage:** a trip by boat
- ⓘ **wall-to-wall:** so crowded there is no extra space
- **yams:** some people call them sweet potatoes

AUTUMN/FALL REVIEW

Answers start on page 192.

CULTURE

Match the special events in the chart to the list below. Write the answer on the line provided.

Labor Day	Columbus Day	Thanksgiving
First Day of School	Election Day	Black Friday
Halloween	Veterans Day	

1. jack-o-lanterns _____

2. voters _____

3. people with a day off from work _____

4. parades _____

5. kids with brand new pencils and notebooks _____

6. turkey _____

7. lots of PIES! _____

8. crowds of shoppers in the mall _____

9. witches _____

10. ceremonies to honor people in the military _____

VOCABULARY

Fall Foods! You know us—we just LOVE to talk about food! (But we'd rather eat it. Haha!) Did we make you as hungry as we made ourselves? How many of these delicious, tasty, sweet, yummy foods have you tried? Can you describe what they are?

11. apples

12. cannoli

13. casserole

14. cranberry sauce

15. gelato

16. gravy

17. pumpkin

18. stuffing

19. candy apple

20. yam

IDIOMATIC EXPRESSIONS

Complete the expressions. What do they mean?

21. She thought the exam would be really hard, but she _____ right through it.

22. In the corn maze, he was completely _____; all the paths looked alike and he had no idea how to escape!

23. He thought the traffic at Thanksgiving would be really bad, but he left early, so it was _____ sailing.

24. Everyone had gone away for the holidays; it was like a(n) _____ town in the office!

25. You didn't study at all for this exam! You don't have a ghost of a(n) _____ to pass!

26. People who want to be politicians need to think about any skeletons they may have in the _____. There are no secrets in politics!

27. Any parent will tell you: Teenagers have HUGE appetites and will _____!

28. I really wanted that third piece of pie, but my eyes were _____ than my stomach. I lifted my fork, but I knew there was no way I could eat it.

29. Thanksgiving is a time when a lot of people _____ out and eat way too much!!

30. I have a lot on my _____ right now. My boss keeps giving me more and more work to do, and I have a lot of responsibilities at home.

ANSWERS
TO
EXERCISES

Winter Section Answers

YOUR TURN: Words that Shine (page 10)

1. sparkled, glittered
2. beaming
3. dazzle
4. flickered
5. gleams
6. flashing
7. glimmering, flickering
8. twinkle
9. glitter
10. glowing
11. glistening

YOUR TURN: Set Phrases with Light Words (page 19)

1. beamed with pride
2. dazzling smile
3. twinkle in his eye; gleam in his eye
4. glittering occasion
5. glistened with tears
6. in glowing terms
7. flashed with anger; glistened with tears
8. glimmer of hope
9. flicker of a frown
10. sparkling wit

YOUR TURN: Symbols of Christmas (page 22)

1. l. mistletoe
2. i. candle

3. k. stocking

4. d. ornament

5. e. fire

6. g. holly

7. a. wreath

8. f. sleigh

9. c. present

10. h. Christmas tree

11. j. snowman

12. b. tree light

YOUR TURN: *-ed* and *-ing* adjectives (page 32)

1. interesting

2. tiring

3. excited

4. amusing

5. encouraged

6. disappointed

7. surprised

8. frightened

9. satisfying

10. confused

YOUR TURN: It's freezing!!! (page 33)

1. f. ear warmer

2. m. fleece

3. i. snowsuit

4. j. jacket

5. l. ski mask

6. o. wool

7. d. beanie

8. a. scarf

9. n. down

10. c. gloves

11. h. ear muffs

12. e. snow pants

13. g. T-shirt and flip-flops

14. k. coat

15. b. mittens

YOUR TURN: Inclusive Language (page 38)

1. actor/actress — actor (yes, for both!)

2. businessman — businessperson

3. chairman — chairperson

4. congressman — congressional representative

5. fireman — firefighter

6. newsman — reporter; newscaster; journalist

7. man-made — artificial; not natural

8. freshman — first-year student

9. mailman — mail carrier

10. host/hostess — host (yes, for both!)

11. spokesman — spokesperson; representative

12. policeman — police officer

13. salesman — sales representative; salesperson

14. waiter/waitress — server

15. weatherman — meteorologist; weather person (Unless the weather is bad. Then blame it on the weather*man*. Haha!)

YOUR TURN: Valentine's Day (page 40)

Things to Say, Write, or Text:

- I love you
- I luv u
- 143 (l = 1; love = 4; 3 = you)
- 1432 (I love you, too)
- mwah! (big smooch!)

Things You Feel:

- love
- a crush on someone
- a broken heart
- excited
- surprised

Things to Give:

- Valentine (card)
- love letter
- flowers
- box of chocolates
- jewelry

Things to Do:

- go to a restaurant (if you like a long wait) OR cook a nice meal
- spend a weekend in the country
- have a couples' spa day
- visit someone who doesn't have a Valentine
- watch a romantic movie at home

CULTURE

1. Yes AND no! (Yes, Jane always keeps her resolutions, but no, Sheila never does! HA—give her another cupcake!)

2. No, George Washington was the first president.

3. No, it celebrates African American culture.

4. No, it's December 25.

5. No, it's celebrated over eight days.

6. No, the date changes, but it will be sometime in late January or early February.

7. No, it means we'll have six more weeks of winter.

8. Yes.

9. No, Christmas Eve is the day before Christmas Day.

10. Yes, Martin Luther King Day is a federal holiday, so most schools are closed.

VOCABULARY

11. blizzard

12. snowdrift

13. snowplows

14. snowman

15. snowsuit

16. gloves

17. sled

18. slush

19. fire

20. hot chocolate

IDIOMATIC EXPRESSIONS

21. f.

22. d.

23. e.

24. j.

25. h.

26. a.

27. c.

28. i.

29. b.

30. g.

Spring Section Answers

YOUR TURN: Foreign Abbreviations (page 55)

1. B.C. or B.C.E
2. A.D. or C.E.
3. vs.
4. i.e.
5. N.B.
6. P.S.
7. etc.
8. e.g.
9. RIP
10. CV

YOUR TURN: Shades of Color (page 60)

Black
- jet
- ebony
- onyx

White
- cream
- ivory
- pearl

Gray
- charcoal
- slate
- silver

Brown
- chocolate
- coffee
- tan

Blue
- indigo
- denim
- navy

Red
- crimson
- ruby
- scarlet

Orange
- apricot
- tangerine
- salmon

Yellow
- mustard
- lemon
- buttercup

Purple
- plum
- lavender
- violet

Pink
- fuchsia
- rose
- blush

Green
- olive
- lime
- mint

YOUR TURN: St Patrick's Day Words (page 62)

1. St. Paddy's Day
2. shamrocks
3. leprechaun
4. rainbow
5. parade
6. famine
7. emerald
8. favor
9. tablecloth
10. corned beef and cabbage with boiled potatoes and Irish soda bread

YOUR TURN: Foreign Expressions (page 71)

1. quid pro quo
2. graffiti
3. mea culpa
4. ad lib
5. paparazzi
6. carpe diem
7. non sequitur
8. carte blanche
9. alumni *or* alumnae *or* alum
10. ciao *or* adios *or* ta ta
11. feng shui
12. caveat
13. ciao *or* adios *or* ta ta *or* bon voyage!
14. résumé (*or* C.V.!)

YOUR TURN: Dressing Up for Mardi Gras (page 72)

1. shampoo
2. conditioner
3. hair dryer
4. toothpaste
5. toothbrush
6. eyebrow pencil
7. lipstick
8. mascara
9. nail polish
10. perfume
11. blush
12. costume

YOUR TURN: Synonyms (page 78)

1. odd
2. shut
3. colleagues
4. huge
5. vacant
6. mistake
7. exit
8. tasty
9. starving
10. hilarious
11. prank
12. cheerful

YOUR TURN: Magic Trick Words (page 80)

1. b.
2. a.
3. h.
4. e.
5. f.
6. c.
7. d.
8. g.

YOUR TURN: Antonyms (page 84)

1. cloudy
2. inside
3. cold
4. ill
5. high
6. dangerous
7. noisy
8. heavy
9. expensive
10. easy

SPRING REVIEW ANSWERS (page 90)

CULTURE

1. Passover
2. Mardi Gras
3. St. Patrick's Day
4. Mardi Gras
5. April Fool's Day

6. Easter

7. Ramadan

8. Cinco de Mayo

9. Easter

10. St. Patrick's Day

VOCABULARY

11. ladybugs

12. mask

13. parades

14. crowds

15. piñata

16. pollen

17. tissues

18. fridge

19. jewelry

20. balloon

IDIOMATIC EXPRESSIONS

21. no spring chicken: not young; old

22. springs up: appears, as a new shop

23. to go green: to become environmentally friendly

24. beginner's luck: doing very well at something you have never done before, especially a sport or game

25. walk on eggshells: be very careful what you say and do so someone doesn't become upset

26. good egg: a kind person

27. make a fool of someone: make someone look silly

28. a laugh a minute: lots of fun

29. throw a party: give a party

30. party pooper: someone who does not like parties and makes everyone else miserable

Summary Section Answers

YOUR TURN: Compound Nouns (page 98)

1. homesick
2. heat wave
3. life-threatening
4. flip-flops
5. water park
6. sunscreen
7. watermelon
8. ice cream
9. sandcastles
10. pocket money

YOUR TURN: *For* and *Since* (page 103)

1. for
2. since
3. for
4. for
5. since
6. for
7. since
8. for
9. since
10. since
11. for
12. for

YOUR TURN: Summer Words (page 105)

1. n.
2. c.
3. l.
4. g.
5. a.
6. h.
7. b.
8. d.
9. k.
10. m.
11. i.
12. j.
13. f.
14. e.

YOUR TURN: Onomatopoeia (page 112)

1. c.
2. e.
3. f.
4. h.
5. i.
6. l.
7. j.
8. a.
9. k.
10. d.
11. g.
12. b.

YOUR TURN: Fourth of July Words (page 113)

1. Independence Day
2. colonies
3. Declaration of Independence
4. fireworks
5. legal
6. parade
7. cookout, barbecue, BBQ, bbq
8. pets/pooches
9. Great Britain
10. cookout, barbecue, BBQ, bbq

YOUR TURN: Abstract Nouns (page 120)

(In the directions, the separated compound nouns to spot are *Las Vegas* and *wedding cake*!)

1. friendship
2. love
3. surprise
4. joy/happiness/excitement
5. anxiety, worry
6. pride
7. relief
8. disbelief/anger
9. creativity
10. anxiety/worry

YOUR TURN: Wedding Words (page 122)

1. d.
2. j.
3. g.

4. h.

5. i.

6. a.

7. f.

8. b.

9. e.

10. c.

SUMMER REVIEW ANSWERS (page 128)

CULTURE

1. False. On Memorial Day we remember those who died while serving their country.

2. True.

3. True.

4. True.

5. False. It celebrates America's freedom from Britain.

6. False. Different states have different laws about fireworks.

7. False. It is the Declaration of Independence.

8. False. The flag does have 50 stars for the 50 states, but it has 13 stripes for the 13 original colonies.

9. True.

10. False. Even if you can't attend, you should reply.

VOCABULARY

11. e.

12. a.

13. j.

14. b.

15. h.

16. g.

17. i.

18. c.

19. d.

20. f.

IDIOMATIC EXPRESSIONS

21. something fishy (People do NOT climb in windows of a bank! It must mean trouble!)

22. make a splash (If people notice how FABULOUS and exciting the product is, the company could sell MILLIONS!)

23. it's no picnic (Doing something under difficult circumstances is very hard.)

24. flag down (It seems that every taxi in the city is in use when it's raining, so waving for one to stop isn't likely to be very successful!)

25. tie the knot (If they get married soon, we can all go to a fun party!)

26. made for each other (Perfect together.)

27. No sweat! (Reading and practice make learning English EASY! Okay, maybe not easy, but lots of fun!)

28. shoot the breeze (They have snacks and just chat about fun things.)

29. Hot dog! (WOW! I'm so excited!)

30. has a crush (Toby thinks he's in love with Celia.)

Autumn/Fall Answers

YOUR TURN: Commonly Confused Words (page 139)

1. capital
2. except
3. affected
4. principal
5. quite
6. stationary
7. complement
8. conscience
9. proceed; quite
10. personal

YOUR TURN: More Commonly Confused Words (page 146)

1. there; It's
2. their; two
3. too
4. there; too
5. it's; their
6. There are
7. to; their
8. They're; to
9. to; too
10. it's

YOUR TURN: Columbus Day True or False (page 148)

1. F (Spain)
2. F (Three ships: the *Niña*, the *Pinta*, and the *Santa Maria*)
3. T

4. F (He arrived at the islands of the Caribbean, but it sure would be funny if he did say that. Haha!)

5. T

6. F (Some people think that soon after Columbus arrived, he and the nations of Europe began to exploit the native peoples and destroy their culture.)

7. T

8. F (the second Monday in October)

9. F (Many government offices are closed, but many businesses are open.)

10. T (TRUE! TRUE! TRUE!)

YOUR TURN: Even More Commonly Confused Words (page 154)

1. Our; Bye

2. our; buy

3. You're; your

4. buy; our

5. your

6. your; buy; our

7. are

8. by

YOUR TURN: Halloween Words (page 156)

1. l.

2. c.

3. g.

4. h.

5. i.

6. j.

7. e.

8. f.

9. d.

10. b.

11. a.

12. k.

YOUR TURN: Using the Word *long* (page 162)

1. come a long way

2. long shot

3. long week

4. So long

5. for the long haul

6. long for

7. a long way

8. in the long run

9. long face

10. long weekend

11. long day

12. take a long look

YOUR TURN: Thanksgiving Words (page 164)

1. Pilgrims

2. set sail

3. Native Americans

4. crops

5. appreciate

6. turkey

7. floats

8. Black Friday

9. doorbusters

10. nap

CULTURE

1. Halloween

2. Election Day

3. Labor Day, *and/or* Columbus Day *and/or* Thanksgiving *and/or* Black Friday

4. Thanksgiving *and/or* Veterans Day

5. first day of school

6. Thanksgiving

7. Thanksgiving

8. Black Friday

9. Halloween

10. Veterans Day

VOCABULARY

11. apples (Oh, come on! This one is easy as, ahem, PIE! Ha, ha!)

12. cannoli: Italian treats made of crisp, flat cookies rolled around cream

13. casserole: a dish prepared from many ingredients (such as meat and vegetables)

14. cranberry sauce: a jelly prepared from cranberries

15. gelato: an Italian ice cream treat

16. gravy: the yummy sauce made from meat juices. Try it on mashed potatoes!

17. pumpkin: large orange fruit (yes! It's a fruit, not a vegetable!) that becomes ripe in fall

18. stuffing: a special dish of bread pieces and seasonings cooked inside a turkey (our favorite!)

19. candy apple: an apple on a stick, covered with caramel or red hard candy

20. yam: often called a sweet potato. YUM—yams!

IDIOMATIC EXPRESSIONS

21. sailed—sail right through something: do something very easily

22. at sea—completely at sea: very confused

23. clear—clear sailing: easy to do, with no problems

24. ghost—ghost town: a town that has no one living there

25. chance—ghost of a chance: no chance at all!

26. closet—skeleton in the closet: a big, bad, embarrassing secret that someone is hiding

27. eat you out of house and home—eat just about everything in the house

28. bigger—my eyes were bigger than my stomach: I took too much food!

29. pig—pig out: eat too much of a favorite food

30. plate—have a lot on your plate: be busy with too many stressful responsibilities

APPENDIX A
AUDIO
TRANSCRIPTS

Winter Audio Dialogues

Introduction

Winter Weather

He: Oh, man, I am freezing! Can't we **turn up** the heat?

She: Oh come on. It's nice and warm in here! Just put on another sweater. It's all about the layers. . .

He: Layers?! Layers?! Are you kidding?! There aren't enough layers in my entire closet to keep me warm today. This **cold snap** is **brutal**. Let's just turn up the heat.

She: You're such a baby.

He: No. If I were a baby I'd have a nice warm snowsuit. And **blankets**. Lots of blankets! And you'd have the HEAT TURNED UP!

She: Hey, what's the **forecast**, anyway? It's bitter cold out there . . . This morning the store was **packed** and a guy said a big snowstorm is coming. There was not even one **loaf** of bread left on the shelf!

He: Yeah, I don't get that. I mean, why do people **stock up on** bread and milk before it snows? *Bread and milk*!? What exactly are people doing with all that bread and milk?!

She: Uh . . . milk . . . sandwiches?

He: Funny. Haha. I guess if people are afraid of being **snowbound**, at least they can have toast. And milk. Haha. I'll tell you this—if I'm ever snowbound, I sure don't want milk and bread. I want pizza and pretzels and ice cream . . . maybe some hot dogs . . .

She: That's all junk food! I guess you've given up on your New Year's resolution to eat healthful foods and lose weight!

He: Eh, I'm not worried. Every year I put on ten pounds of **winter weight**, and I always lose it by summer. So, **I figure** if I'm snowbound, I might as well enjoy it.

She: Stop, don't even say it! I think I'll go crazy if we're snowbound. I've already got **cabin fever** from being **stuck in the house** all winter. If we're snowed in, I'll really be **climbing the walls**.

He: Well, think about this . . . If we get stuck in the house, we'll have lots of time to plan.

She: Ummm . . . . Plan what?

He: Our next fun winter activity!

She: Oh boy . . . You mean freezing outside to build a snowman?

He: Uh, no . . .

She: Sledding down the hill in town?

He: Nope.

She: Okay, okay, just tell me what this big winter plan is!

He: A CARIBBEAN ISLAND VACATION! Sunshine! Beaches! Warm weather! Fruity drinks with little umbrellas!

She: That's your big plan?

He: That's my big plan.

She: **In your dreams**. I'll go turn up the heat . . .

VOCABULARY

- **blankets:** the very large pieces of warm fabric on your bed (or sofa) to keep you warm
- **brutal:** an adjective in a set phrase, like *bitter cold*, to describe extremely cold weather or winds (*This cold is brutal. These winds are brutal.*)
- ⓘ **cabin fever:** the feeling of not being able to go out of the house for activities because of cold weather
- ⓘ **climbing the walls:** the feeling of being so bored you think you'll go crazy!
- **cold snap:** a sudden period of really cold weather
- **forecast:** prediction about the weather
- ⓘ **I figure:** I think
- **in your dreams:** haha, it will never happen!
- **loaf:** a single quantity of bread—one large piece, or sliced
- ⓘ **packed:** really, *really* crowded
- **snowbound:** not able to go out easily because of weather; stuck in the house
- **stock up on:** get a supply of something so you have a lot of it
- ⓘ **stuck in the house:** not able to go out easily because of weather
- **turn up:** increase; raise; make higher (as volume or *heat*!)
- **winter weight:** those extra pounds you gain from sitting around the house because it's too cold to go out for exercise and activities!

Classic Movies

He: Hey, what's your favorite holiday movie?

She: Oh boy . . . it's hard to say. I like to watch a **bunch of** them around the holidays. What's your favorite?

He: I have to say my favorite is *A Christmas Carol*. All those ghosts visiting Mr. Scrooge, showing him his future if he doesn't change his mean ways . . . It's kind of heartwarming. Scrooge doesn't care about anything but money in the beginning, but at the end he's kind and generous, and everyone is happy. Yeah, *A Christmas Carol* is my favorite.

She: Hmm. That reminds me of *Dr. Seuss's How the Grinch Stole Christmas*. That mean old Grinch hated to see people so happy . . . so he stole all their holiday stuff . . . but they were STILL happy! It wasn't about the "stuff"! And then the Grinch **changed his ways**, and had a happier heart . . . . Now that's a nice holiday message for everyone.

He: I agree. They're both heartwarming movies.

She: And then there's my other favorite—the one with the wacky family trying to have a nice holiday . . . with cranky teenagers, and goofy cousins, and that funny grandma, and the cat that bites the string of lights, and the dad who wants to make it a PERFECT holiday for everyone . . .

He: HA—NATIONAL LAMPOON'S CHRISTMAS VACATION! Such a funny movie!

She: Yeah, so funny! And my favorite character is the **delivery boy** . . . Remember that part where he **rings the doorbell** and the dad opens the door, and the delivery boy is standing in the snow and he says: "I was supposed to deliver it yesterday, but it fell between the seats and I didn't see it . . . I'm sorry." And the door goes **SLAM**! "Merry Chris . . . mas." HA! I just love that!

He: Hmm. Could it be that he's your favorite character because he also happens to be your . . . brother?

She: Well, yes, there's that . . . but come on, admit it. That's a funny movie.

He: Yeah, yeah it is pretty funny. But you know what the best part is of watching all these movies?

She: Um. . . a heartwarming holiday theme?

He: Yes . . . and . . .?

She: Interesting characters?

He: Yes . . . and . . .?

She: Hmm. Movies and . . .???

He: Movies and . . .

Both: POPCORN!

VOCABULARY

- **bunch of:** lots of; many
- **change one's ways:** decide to behave differently
- **delivery boy:** person hired to bring mail, packages, or messages from a company
- **ring the doorbell:** push the button at someone's door to make a sound inside the house so they know you're there!
- **SLAM!:** the sound a door makes when someone closes it in a very loud way; it's onomatopoeia!

AUDIO TRACK 4

Visiting the City

He: Hey, I was talking to my **buddy** Michael today. School's out for a two-week **winter break** around the holidays, so he and Justine are taking the kids to see the tree at **Rockefeller Center**.

She: Wow, New York City during the holidays! I can't think of anything more beautiful! I grew up in the city, and I still remember my mom taking us to see *The Nutcracker* at **Lincoln Center**. We went every year—it was our holiday tradition! I still remember how much I loved the lights, and the decorations, and all the holiday sounds. It's such a magical time for kids.

He: I went in to the city once at the holidays. That was enough for me. Yeah, it's pretty, and there are lots of special holiday events, but I just remember freezing! I think the temperature was **minus 3 degrees** with the **wind chill**!

She: I guess we were lucky. My dad would drive, and drop us off right at the door. We'd hurry inside while he figured out where to park the car.

He: Ha—your dad was a *saint* to drive through that mess of **nightmare** traffic! And parking?! Ha, finding a parking spot—THAT would be a Christmas miracle!

She: I know! When I think of it now . . . .! And then he'd drive us to see the department store windows—every year the holiday scenes were better than the last—we kids loved that.

He: Well, I'm pretty sure Michael plans to take the subway. That's a big

adventure for the kids. And it's an **easy walk** to Rockefeller Center from the subway station. Well . . . easy, if it's not a zero-degree day!

She: Hey, kids bundle up. They don't feel the cold; only cranky old people like you complain about the cold. The tree at Rockefeller Center is always so beautiful—and maybe the kids will be able to **ice skate** at the **rink**!

He: Are you kidding?! Those kids will be lucky to get a **glimpse** of the tree. Last time I went, there were hundreds of people, all crowding around to see the tree, and the ice skaters, and take pictures. I was glad to get out of there without being **crushed**!

She: Yeah, I know the city can be pretty **crazy** around the holidays . . . But **it's worth it** to me. Happy Holidays, Tim!

He: Bah humbug!

VOCABULARY

- **adventure:** a really exciting activity
- ⓘ **buddy:** a good friend
- ⓘ **crazy:** wild, exciting (in a good OR bad way!)
- **crushed:** pushed really tightly; in a crowd, pressed very tightly among people
- **easy walk:** not far; a short distance
- **glimpse:** see very quickly
- **ice skate:** put on special shoe-like boots with blades and slide across the ice
- **it's worth it:** *It may be difficult, but the result makes me happy, so I'm glad to do it!*
- **Lincoln Center:** a famous performing arts theater in NYC
- **minus (some number) degrees:** below zero degrees F. *brrrrrrr!*
- **nightmare:** a bad dream; a very bad or complicated situation
- **rink:** a large area of ice for ice skating
- **Rockefeller Center:** a famous landmark in NYC
- ⓘ **saint:** a really, *really* good person
- **wind chill:** a wind effect that makes the temperature seem even colder
- **winter break:** a time around the holidays when most schools are closed for a week or two

Returns

Guy: Hey, so have you finished your holiday shopping?

Girl: Yeah, I figure I'm as finished as I'll ever be. I think I found something for everyone on my list.

Guy: Wow, so now you can relax and just enjoy the holidays without all the crowds at the mall. Nice!

Girl: Not exactly. I bought a beautiful wool scarf for my nephew Jeremy, and I just remembered that he's **allergic** to wool!

Guy: Ooh. Not good. So you're worried that when he wears the scarf he'll break out in an **itchy rash**?

Girl: Are you kidding? I can't give him that scarf! I don't want him to think I'm trying to make him **miserable**! "Oh, happy holidays, Jeremy—here's a present that will make you itchy and uncomfortable." **No way**! I have to return it. I'll find something less . . . uh, dangerous to give him.

Guy: Haha, so it's back to the mall for you.

Girl: Yeah, but I think I'll wait until after the holidays. I bought it at Martin's Department Store, and they have a really good returns policy. I can **take it back** any time before January 30th, and they'll give me a full refund as long as I have the receipt. Which I do.

Guy: Hey, that's good to know. Martin's is a pretty fancy store—I thought they'd only make an **even exchange** or give you a store credit. Which isn't really a problem, because it's easy to find something really nice at Martin's. I'd spend that store credit in ten minutes!

Girl: Well, I'll be glad to have the refund in January, because that's when all my holiday shopping credit card bills will be coming in.

Guy: Well, you still have the problem of finding a gift for Jeremy that won't have him itching and scratching in misery . . .

Girl: And I just figured it out! I'll give him a gift card to Martin's!

VOCABULARY

- **allergic:** having a reaction to something, like pollen in the air, or some fabrics
- **even exchange:** bringing back an item to a store, and getting the same item in a different color or size
- **itchy:** the painful feeling of needing to scratch or rub a place on the skin
- **miserable:** very, *very* uncomfortable; in pain
- ⓘ **no way!:** *haha, it will never happen!* or *you're kidding!*
- **rash:** redness or itchy spots on the skin
- **take something back:** return an item to the store where you bought it

AUDIO TRACK 6

Chocolate!

She: Yay, it's almost Valentine's Day!

He: Valentine's Day . . . I guess you're expecting a card and flowers.

She: Oh. Well yeah, that would be nice. But I'm not expecting a card or flowers.

He: Oh boy. I guess that means you're hoping for some jewelry . . .

She: Oh. Well I would never **turn down** a pretty gold bracelet or silver chain . . . But I'm not expecting jewelry.

He: Hmm. No card. No flowers. No jewelry. Doesn't that about cover the typical Valentine's presents?

She: I think you forgot one . . . Here's a hint: Comes in a big red box . . . . Has a big red bow . . . Lots of little treats inside . . .

He: OF COURSE! How could I forget the classic present: a big box of chocolates! So on Valentine's Day you will have a big box of your favorite candy, right?

She: Almost right. Actually I really love Valentine's Day because of the day after it . . . ! On February 15th I'll head to the store and stock up on my favorite beautiful boxes of chocolate—at **HALF-PRICE**! I'll sit on the sofa and watch romantic movies, and eat bargain chocolate, and think about how much I love the day AFTER Valentine's Day!

He: Ha—pretty smart! But what about your New Year's resolution? I thought you were going to lose weight. I thought you were going to quit junk food.

She: Well I am. But haven't you been keeping up with the news? Don't you check all the Good Health websites? Chocolate is GOOD for you! It has all kinds of benefits for your health! Chocolate is a health food! In fact, now that

I think about it, maybe I shouldn't wait until after Valentine's Day . . . Maybe I should hurry up and eat some chocolate immediately . . . For my health, of course.

He: For your health, of course . . .

VOCABULARY

- **half-price:** 50% less than it cost before!
- **turn down:** say no to something; or, make lower (as volume, or heat!)

Spring Audio Dialogues

Mow the Lawn!

He: Well, looks like I won't be mowing the lawn this afternoon. Let's go to a movie.

She: whoa, whoa, whoa . . . . What do mean you *won't* be mowing the lawn? The grass is growing! It's spring! It's Saturday! It's your JOB to mow the lawn on Saturday in spring!

He: Yeah, yeah yeah, I know, I know. And I love to mow the lawn, I really do. I love the smell of the fresh-cut grass, and I love the cool breeze . . . . .

She: OH PLEASE! fresh-cut grass . . . cool breeze . . . You're just hoping to **hire** the kid next door to do it for you!

He: You know me so well . . . . But really, no kidding! I can't mow the lawn this afternoon. Didn't you hear the weather report? There's a chance of rain! Can't mow the grass in the rain.

She: Hey, you! It's SPRING. There's ALWAYS a chance of rain. Get out there and start up the lawnmower.

He: But it's **partly** cloudy . . .

She: Partly? PARTLY!? It's *partly* cloudy? Well, then, what's the other part?

He: Umm . . .

She: Exactly. Partly cloudy, so the other part is SUNNY.

He: But, umm . . .

She: Oh. wait . . . . .. Great.

He: What?

She: Look out the window. We've been talking about the weather for so long that it's started to drizzle . . . . There goes the lawnmowing . . .

He: YAY! Like I said, Let's go to a movie!

VOCABULARY

- **hire:** pay someone to do a job
- **partly:** not completely

Crazy-ish Plans

He: Hey, do you **feel like** going to a movie tonight?

She: Yeah, that sounds like a great idea. What time were you thinking?

He: I don't know . . . How does 5-ish sound? We can have something to eat before we go.

She: Well, 5-ish sounds okay to me. But can we finish eating before the movie starts?

He: Sure! We should be finished with dinner . . . oh, 7-ish.

She: Okay, but, um, what time is the movie?

He: Well, I didn't actually check the time, but it's probably around 8-ish. I think.

She: Oh boy. This whole idea is starting to sound a little crazy-ish. I think I'll skip the movie and **color** my hair tonight instead.

He: WHAT?! You color your hair???? But it looks so . . . so . . . so natural. –ish.

She: Oh very funny. Maybe I'll really go crazy and pick a new color. I'm tired of being a brunette. I'm thinking blonde! A nice, warm champagne blonde.

He: Ooooh. That sounds TERRIBLE.

She: WHAT? Why? Come on, admit it—it's better than gray. I mean gray-ish.

He: No, the blonde sounds okay to me . . .

She: Then what's the problem?

He: WARM CHAMPAGNE IS THE PROBLEM! eeeeww!!!! If you're going for champagne, it should be ice cold!

She: Oh boy . . . .

VOCABULARY

- **color:** use a dye to change hair color
- **feel like:** want to do something

Jewelry Store

She: oooh, look at that **gorgeous** bracelet . . . .

He: How did this happen?

She: Um, how did what happen?

He: How did we end up looking in the window of a jewelry store at the MALL??? I thought we were going to the movies.

She: Oh come on. We'll see the movie. But we're a little too early, so . . . . .

He: So . . . **Plan B** is Go Jewelry Shopping?

She: Well, it is my birthday next week . . . .

He: Oh. And you were hoping to get a gold bracelet or necklace?

She: Well . . . .

He: A pretty ring?

She: Hmmm . . . .

He: Some new gold earrings?

She: Oh, I just know that anything you pick will be perfect!

He: Well I am so glad that you just said that . . . because now I know you'll love the perfect new . . . lawnmower I picked for you! Happy Birthday!

VOCABULARY

- **gorgeous:** really, *really*, beautiful
- ⓘ **Plan B:** what you do if you can't do what you *first* wanted to do!

AUDIO TRACK 10

Just an Omelet

Server: Good morning, welcome to Pop's Diner. Can I get you some coffee? Oh, and I'll bring you a menu.

Customer: Coffee, yes. But I don't think I need a menu. I'll just have an omelet.

Server: Are you sure? We have a pretty big menu...

Customer: **Nah**, no I don't need a menu. Just an omelet please.

Server: Okaaay. What kind of omelet do you want?

Customer: Hmm. Oh, just a cheese omelet. With ham.

Server: What kind of cheese—American, cheddar, swiss, Monterey Jack, feta, or goat cheese?

Customer: Ummm. uhhhh . . . .. American, I guess.

Server: The American cheese omelet comes with onions, **spinach**, mushrooms, or kale.

Customer: Ummmm . . . . No, no vegetables for me. Just the cheese.

Server: Okay, do you still want it with ham?

Customer: Yes. Just the cheese. No vegetables. And yes, ham.

Server: What kind of ham—country, spiced, black forest, honey, baked, smoked, glazed, Virginia, Taylor? Or ham steak?

Customer: Ummm . . . .. uhhhhhh . . . . Hey, you know I think I changed my mind. I'll just have some eggs.

Server: soft-boiled, poached, **Eggs Benedict**, fried, over-easy, scrambled, or just egg whites?

Customer: *aaaaarghhhh*!

VOCABULARY

- **Eggs Benedict:** breakfast dish of poached (cooked in water) eggs, ham, and Hollandaise sauce (Don't ask us—it's a fancy cooking word!) on an English muffin (a special round bread). WE WANT THIS NOW!!!
- ℹ️ **nah:** a very informal *no*
- **spinach:** a leafy green vegetable (Hey, this is one that we actually like!)

AUDIO TRACK 11

April Fool

He: Hey, don't forget to print that report for the meeting this morning.

She: WHAT???? Wait, what report?

He: Wow, it's the one the boss asked you for . . . the sales report. We've got a meeting in an hour, and he needs it!

She: NO!!!! No, no, no, no! No, that report isn't due for a month . . . on the first.

He: My, my, my . . . Do you see the big 1 on the calendar? Today IS the first!

She: But wait! No, I thought the boss meant the first of NEXT month!

He: Hoo boy. NO, it's today and the big boss from headquarters is coming down just for our meeting.

She: Oh NO! What am I going to do? I haven't even started that report! The boss is going to kill me! Oh no. Nonononononno . . .

He: Whoa! Whoa*whoa*whoa*whoa* . . . .

She: What?

He: Look carefully at the calendar. Yeah, it IS the first today, but it's the first of

April . . . APRIL FOOL!

She: Oh man!!!!! Wow, you really got me that time! I was really in a panic.

He: Haha, I know! I was going to keep the joke going a little longer, but you really did look worried!

She: WORRIED?! No, that was PANIC!

He: HA! Well, I guess I got you back for last year . . . Remember last April Fool's Day when you made me believe the boss was going to fire me?

She: HAHA, oh yeah . . . That really was a good one, wasn't it? Okay, I guess I deserved this, didn't I?

He: Um, yes. Yes you did!

She: Just you wait for next year . . .

AUDIO TRACK 12

Do it Yourself!

Store Guy: Hi. Can I help you find something?

Customer: I hope so. I want a mirror with a pretty **frame** around it.

Store Guy: We have a bunch of mirrors over in **Aisle** 5. On the left side.

Customer: Yeah, I looked at those. There are some really nice ones, but they're pretty expensive. Actually, I have a plain mirror at home, and I thought maybe I could just make a frame for it.

Store Guy: Oh. Yeah, I think you should be able to do that. You'd just need to buy some **molding** and special glue. Maybe some paint . . .

Customer: YES! That is exactly what I was thinking! But I could use some help with HOW to do it.

Store Guy: We have a pretty big Do It Yourself section. Lots of people find help with their DIY projects there. Check Aisle 14. You can find DIY kits with everything you need, or just instructions for the Do It Yourself project you're planning.

Customer: Aisle 14?

Store Guy: Yeah. **You can't miss it**. There's a big sign that says, "DIY" right at the front of the aisle.

Customer: Thanks a lot!

Store Guy: Good luck.

VOCABULARY

- **aisle:** the walkway between all the stuff in a store
- **frame:** wood or metal pieces going around a picture or mirror
- **molding:** (sometimes spelled *moulding*) wood pieces used to frame pictures, and to decorate walls near ceilings
- **you can't miss it:** There are very large or very clear signs to show you where something is.

Summer Audio Dialogues

School's Out

She: Uh, hey, that's a pretty happy look on your face. I wonder what that could mean . . .

He: Ha—you know exactly what it means! School's out for the summer! *"No more pencils, no more books. No more teachers' dirty looks!"*

She: Um... Wait. You *are* a teacher. And **what the heck** are "dirty looks" anyway?

He: Yeah, yeah, yeah, I'm a teacher. But when there's no school, I just like to dream that I will never have to sharpen another pencil again. EVER!

She: You are too funny. But wait. If I remember correctly, it's the students, not the teachers, who do all the pencil sharpening. So, anyway . . . what about those "dirty looks"?

He: Ha! Come on, you know that look I mean . . . It's the "Little Johnny and Susie didn't do their homework or their summer reading" look. *grrrrrrrrrrr*

VOCABULARY

ⓘ **what the heck:** a silly exclamation of surprise

Play Ball!

He: Okay, what's your favorite part of the baseball game? Is it when the **batter** hits the ball, and the team scores a **run**?

She: Hmm. A run is nice . . . um, if it's my home team that gets it!

He: Uh, okay, well then is it when the batter on the other team **strikes out**?

She: Hmm . . . that's nice too.

He: Then it must be when you hear the **umpire** yell, "**SAFE!**" when your favorite player runs to **home plate**.

She: Nice, but not my favorite part of the game.

He: Okay, I give up. Please tell me your favorite part of the baseball game.

She: Well, you know that part of the game when everyone stands up to sing "Take Me Out to the Ballgame"?

He: Of course—so singing during the **seventh inning stretch** is your favorite part of the game!

She: Close. But it's not the singing that I like. It's heading to the snack area for hot dogs while everyone *else* is singing . . . that's what I like!

VOCABULARY

- **batter:** the player trying to hit the baseball
- **home plate:** where the batters stand as they try to hit the ball. They return here to score a *run*.
- **run:** when a baseball player scores! (a run = a point in scoring)
- **safe:** The player made it to a *base* or *home* without the other team stopping him.
- **seventh inning stretch:** a time in the baseball game when most of the people stand up, relax, and sing the traditional baseball song, "Take Me Out to the Ballgame"
- **strikes out:** misses hitting the ball three times
- **umpire:** the person who decides if a play in the game can count

AUDIO TRACK 15

Lemonade Stand

She: Hey, aren't those kids just so cute? Look at them with their little cups and that big **pitcher** of lemonade. Come on, let's go buy some lemonade. Only ten cents!

He: Are you kidding?! Those kids are like professional business **executives**! Sure, they may look cute, but it's all a trick!

She: Oh, come on. Look at those little faces! They probably worked all morning, **squeezing** lemons, stirring sugar . . . Come on, only ten cents!

He: HAH! You think those little kids made all that lemonade?! I bet those little kids were playing video games while *Mom* made all that lemonade.

She: Oh stop it. They're cute little kids trying to keep busy and earn some pocket money during the summer. I'm going to buy us both a cup of lemonade. Can you give me a dollar?

He: But the lemonade's only ten cents!

She: Well I'm going to give them a dollar.

He: YOU SEE WHAT I MEAN?! They look cute, but it's all a TRICK!!!

VOCABULARY

- **executives:** very important people in a company
- **pitcher:** a large container for pouring cold drinks
- **squeeze:** put pressure on something; using hands or a kitchen device, putting pressure on fruit lets the juice come out

AUDIO TRACK 16

Memorial Day Weekend

Guy: Hey Lana, what's with the beach towel and flip-flops?

Girl: Are you kidding? Don't you know what weekend this is?!

Guy: Ummm . . . .

Girl: Come on . . . . Think about it . . . Monday is the last Monday of May. Does that ring a bell?

Guy: Ummm . . . .

Girl: Last Monday in May . . . .? Three day weekend . . . ?? Flags . . . ? Parades . . . .? No school. No work . . .

Guy: Wait! I've got it! It's Memorial Day Weekend! Wow, how could I forget that? My grandfather served in the military, and he died in battle. Of course I remember Memorial Day. I'm so proud that everyone takes a day to honor those who died for our country.

Girl: I knew you wouldn't forget such an important national holiday.

Guy: Of course not! In fact, I'm going to the cemetery with some volunteers. We'll put American flags on the graves of people who died fighting for our country in war. I'm proud to remember them.

Girl: Yes, and then we can watch the parade in town. I'm ready to wave the Stars and Stripes!

Guy: Yeah, but what about the beach towel and flip-flops . . . ?

Girl: Ummm . . . . Memorial Day is a holiday of remembrance . . . but it's also the unofficial FIRST DAY OF SUMMER!

Guy: Oh boy. I guess that means traffic jams on the turnpike. Oh well, SUNNYSIDE BEACH, HERE WE COME!

Girl: Hmm. Yeah. Us . . . . . . and three million other people.

Fireworks

She: Hey, let's get some fireworks for the 4th of July cookout.

He: What?! We can't get fireworks! They're illegal in this state!

She: Wait. I'm talking about those little fireworks things shaped like a round-ish stick and covered with paper . . . You know, you light them with a match and they start to burn, and then something shoots up into the sky.

He: They're called Roman candles. And they're not legal.

She: Hmm . . . Well, how about some firecrackers? You know, those little things you light, and they go *CRACK, crack crack*!?

He: Illegal.

She: Wait. What? Even those sparkly little sticks that give off tiny sparks when we wave them around in our hands? What do they call those little sparkly sticks anyway?

He: Um, those little sparkly sticks are called sparklers. And they are illegal.

She: Oh come on, . . . Really? But those sparkly little sticks look so pretty at night!

He: Well, I hope you enjoy looking at them now. Because, in this state, if the police see you waving those pretty little sparklers, you could have to pay a fine of $500. Or go to jail for 30 days! And anyone who sells those pretty little sparklers could go to jail for *18 months*! You won't be seeing pretty little sparkly sticks in jail, that's for sure.

She: But that's just crazy. If I drive across the bridge into the next state, there are tons of stores that sell fireworks! I could even buy my sparklers at the supermarket!

He: Yeah, in that state sparklers and small fireworks are legal. You can wave your little sparkly stick all you want! But big firecrackers that explode in the air are NOT legal.

She: Wait. So Roman candles are NOT legal in that state but the sparklers *are*?

He: Right. And it's not legal to *have* them, but it *is* legal to *sell* them.

She: *AAAARRRGHHHH!* About the only thing that's going to explode now is my HEAD!!!!

RSVP

She: Wow, this is a surprise. We got an invitation to my boss's wedding. I didn't expect that.

He: Really? I thought she was having a very small wedding—just a short church ceremony for very close friends and family.

She: Yeah, that's what I thought, too. Do you think she includes me in her "very close friends" list? We really only work together . . . . We don't really **socialize** outside of work.

He: Well, she must think you're special if you got an invitation . . .

She: But this may be a little **awkward**. If I **mention** that I got an invitation, all the other people in the office may feel disappointed. I think I'd feel really uncomfortable letting them know that the boss thinks I'm a special friend.

He: Well, just don't mention it at work. Is there a response card in the invitation?

She: **Of course**. And it requests that all guests RSVP as soon as possible. I'm sure they need a **head count** to plan for dinner.

He: Well, just send back the response and don't say anything about it at work.

She: Yeah, that sounds like the best thing to do. I don't want anyone to know the boss thinks I'm the only one in the office special enough to invite to her wedding.

****************** *the next day* ****************

He: Well? How did it go today? Were you able to keep your invitation a secret? Or did you **spill the beans**?

She: No, I didn't spill the beans. I didn't even mention the wedding.

He: Perfect! Then no one knows that the boss thinks you're special enough to get an invitation to her wedding!

She: Well, not exactly . . .

He: What do you mean? Someone knows that you're invited?

She: Um, yeah, I guess you could say that.

He: But if you didn't say anything about it, how could they know that you got an invitation?

She: Because the guy at the desk next to mine said to the whole room, "Hey! I got an invitation to the boss's wedding! I guess I'm special!"

He: Oh no. Did everyone feel bad that they were **left out**?

She: Not exactly . . .

He: What do you mean?

She: Well, as soon as he said that, everyone in the office said, "Me too!" EVERYONE in the office got an invitation!

He: Haha! Well, I'm sure you're special—but so are the twenty other people you work with!

VOCABULARY

- **awkward:** very uncomfortable in a social situation
- (i) **head count:** the number of people who will be attending an event
- **left out:** not included
- **mention:** say; tell
- **of course:** Sure! Exactly what someone would expect.
- **socialize:** meet as friends just for fun
- (i) **spill the beans:** tell a secret

Autumn/Fall Audio Dialogues

Flavor of the Month!

Barista: Hi. What can I get for you?

He: Coffee.

Barista: Um. Yes. We're a coffee shop . . . . What would you like?

He: Uh . . . coffee . . . ?

Barista: Hot or iced? Super, medium, or regular? **Creamer**? Dairy or non-dairy? **Soy** or milk? Half and half, or cream? Black? **Shot** of flavor or regular? **Foam** or no foam?

He: Whoa whoa whoa . . . . flavor? FLAVOR? Um . . . isn't *coffee* a flavor??

Barista: It's November, sir. We're featuring our special flavo of the month. It's pumpkin. Everyone loves it.

He: Wait wait wait . . . . You mean people want coffee to taste like pumpkin???? And isn't pumpkin a vegetable? Do people want vegetable-tasting coffee????

Barista: Oh sir, you're so funny. It doesn't actually taste like pumpkin. And, um, I think pumpkins are actually considered fruit. But it doesn't really taste like pumpkin anyway. It tastes more like the other things that *flavor* the pumpkin.

He: Wait wait wait. So people want coffee, but they want it to taste like pumpkin, but they don't want it to actually taste like an actual pumpkin, so they add flavors and other spices so it tastes like something else?!

Barista: EXACTLY! And it's our flavor of the month! Everyone LOVES it!

He: *aaaarghhhhh!!!!!* You know, I think I'll just have tea.

Barista: Hot or iced? Herbal or regular? Green or black? India or China? Lemon or milk?

He: *AAAAAAAAAAHHHHHHHH!!!!!!!!!!!!*

VOCABULARY

- **barista:** a person who works in a coffee shop prepairing special coffee drinks
- **creamer:** a substitute for milk to put in coffee

- **foam:** a topping of white bubbles; usually made by a machine that whips the milk
- **shot:** a small amount of sweet flavor added to coffee
- **soy milk:** liquid made from water and soybeans. ICK. (but healthy)

AUDIO TRACK 20

Fall Foliage

He: I'm so glad we have a long weekend later this month. Let's do something different. How about going away?

She: Great idea! This is the perfect time to go to the mountains . . . the leaves are changing colors . . . the weather is cool but still nice . . . the scenery will be gorgeous.

He: You know, we always *talk* about doing this, but we never actually do it. Okay, let's make a plan!

She: I guess we should decide where we want to go first. I vote for New England. Vermont is beautiful all year, but in fall it will be spectacular!

He: Yeah, Vermont is beautiful, and we've never been to the Green Mountains. And umm . . . . You know my favorite ice cream is made in Vermont. Beautiful mountains and mountains of ice cream—YAY what could be better?!

She: Right! I forgot about that! Ha—you just want to go visit the ice cream place for the free samples!

He: Well, I do like to try all the new flavors. And of course it's November, and you know what that means for ice cream . . . .

She: aaaaaargghhhh! Pumpkin! Pumpkinpumpkinpumpkin! I want ice cream that tastes like ice cream, not a vegetable!

He: Pumpkin is a fruit.

She: Yeah, well, **whatever** . . . It's not a fruit I want to eat in my ice cream! And anyway, I thought we were going to see the foliage, not eat ice cream.

He: Yeah, you're right. And you know what? We only have one extra day for this long weekend. If we go to Vermont we'll be spending more time driving in the car on the highway than enjoying the mountain scenery. Maybe we should go someplace a little closer to home.

She: You know, I think you're right. The whole plan is to drive . . . but to drive in the countryside, looking at the fall colors, and taking pictures of the trees and the mountains. Who wants pictures of speeding cars and trucks on the highway?! I think I have a solution: Let's go to the Catskills. I love those mountains, and they're only a three-hour drive away. And Rusty and Rox stayed at a pretty Bed & Breakfast that I think I'd like to try.

He: Sounds like a great idea. Okay, let's call and see if we can get a reservation for the weekend. But remind me—what's the difference between a hotel and a Bed & Breakfast?

She: Oh, a B&B is much nicer than a hotel. It's like a **cozy** country inn owned by really friendly people who usually live right there. It's much more personal than a hotel. The rooms are simple, but very comfortable and beautifully decorated . . . and in the morning the owners serve a delicious home-cooked breakfast, with everything you can think of. And eggs, of course.

He: Okay, it's a plan! Let's call the B&B right now. But if the breakfast is fried eggs with *pumpkin*, I'm **outta** there!

VOCABULARY

- **cozy:** warm and comfortable
- ⓘ **outta:** out of; "I'm outta here" = "I'm leaving . . . NOW!"
- ⓘ **whatever . . . :** it doesn't matter to me; I don't care . . .

AUDIO TRACK 21

Trick or Treat!

The words are "trick or treat." In kid language they mean "Please give us candy, or we will play a trick on you." (The kids don't really play tricks—If you don't have a treat, they just go to the next house!)

So when that doorbell rings, and little ghosts and monsters are hoping for candy, what you will hear is "TRICKATREAT!" It sounds like one (very excited!) word.

AUDIO TRACK 22

Turkey and a Nap!

He: **Holy cow**, I'm stuffed!

She: I'm pretty full, too, but yeah, you sure did seem to . . . . hmm, how can I put this? . . . . you sure did seem to *enjoy* your dinner!

He: Aw, come on. It's Thanksgiving! It's my JOB to eat, eat, then eat some more!

She: Well, you deserve a **promotion** on that job, that's for sure. Because you sure did eat, eat, eat!

He: Come on—didn't you taste those mashed potatoes?! With butter? And salt? So creamy and delicious. Yum.

She: Okay, okay. Yeah, I really liked the mashed potatoes, too. Was that your favorite dish?

He: Hmm. Yeah, probably. But I guess I have to say that the *turkey* was my favorite.

She: Wait, what? What do you mean you "have to say"???

He: Well— I have to say the turkey, because that will explain why I *need* to have a nap . . . . RIGHT NOW!

She: Oh sure, you *need* to have a nap . . . . So I guess you're not sleepy because of all that food you ate . . . I guess you plan to blame it on the tryptophan in the turkey!?

He: **[SNORE]** *ZZZZZZZZZZZZZZZZZZZZZZ*

VOCABULARY

ⓘ **holy cow!:** an exclamation to express surprise or excitement. WOW!
* **promotion:** a better job at work
* **snore:** the sound he (but never *we*!) makes when he's sleeping!

AUDIO TRACK 23

Think About It

He: I'm really looking forward to Thanksgiving. It's my favorite holiday. One day in the year when the most important thing we think about is being thankful.

She: Who are you kidding? I'm pretty sure there's another thing you think about on Thanksgiving . . .

He: Oh, well, yeah of course—family. But that's part of the thankfulness! I'm glad to have a day to just spend time with this big crazy family that I love so much.

She: Okay, but that's not what I was thinking of either. I'm pretty sure there's another thing you think about . . . . . .

He: Being thankful . . . . being with family . . . . What else is there? Oh wait. Yeah yeah yeah. You're talking about football, aren't you?

She: Well, let's see. There's thankful . . . family . . . football . . . .and FOOD! Come on, you know that's your favorite food day of the year.

He: **Very funny.** But, actually I guess it's true. I love ALL the traditional

Thanksgiving foods. No fancy stuff with French names. Just traditional recipes of simple foods. Yum, I can taste the mashed potatoes and gravy now! And anyway, how about *you*? Sometimes I think you try to finish dinner early just so you can get started planning your Black Friday shopping.

She: Not this year. I've been thinking about all those stores that keep opening in the middle of the night. What about the people who work there? Those people have to finish Thanksgiving dinner, leave their families, then hurry in to work. They have to WORK! And now some stores are opening on Thanksgiving Day. So store people have to WORK on Thanksgiving Day. I just don't think it's fair. And I don't think stores should be so concerned with money money money that they won't even close one day for such a special holiday.

He: You're right. I can't believe I'm hearing you say you don't want to go shopping, but you're right.

She: Well, I didn't actually say I don't want to go shopping . . .

He: Oh. You mean you'll just wait until the next day to **hit the mall** in town?

She: No. I mean I'll sit on the sofa and shop at my favorite mall: www.com!

VOCABULARY

ⓘ **hit the mall:** go shopping at the mall

• **very funny:** when said in a slow way, this usually means the opposite— *NOT* very funny!

APPENDIX B
VOCABULARY

blockbuster, 99
blooming, 56
bobbing, 158
boiled, 75
boiling, 116
book a stay, 99
bored, 100
borhani, 125
borrow, 125
boughs, 25
bouquet, 44
break the laws, 116
breeze, 100
bridal party, 125
bride, 125
bridesmaid, 125
Bridezilla, 125
brilliant, 12
brownies, 25
brutal, 198
bubbly, 12
buddy, 201
bumpy, 140
bunch of, 44, 200
bundle up, 12
burger, 116
burrow, 12
buzz, 100
by heart, 25

C

cabbage, 65
cabin fever, 198
calm down, 125
campfire, 100
camp out, 100
candidate, 140
candy apple, 158
candy canes, 25
cannoli, 150

caramel, 44
cards, 56
care package, 100
carol, 25
carry-on bag, 140
cartoon character, 158
carve, 140
casserole, 166
casual, 108
catch, 12
catch up on, 100
celebrity, 150
celery, 75
cemetery, 108
century, 150
ceremony, 125
championship, 12
chances are, 12
change one's ways, 200
change the subject, 150
chaotic, 166
charge, 108
charity, 12
check, 100
checking off, 25
check on, 100
cheering, 12
chemical waste, 158
chicks, 75
chill, 116, 140
chirping, 56
choke, 75
chopped, 75
chores, 100
Christmas list, 25
chubby, 25
chunk, 116
chuppah, 125
city council, 140
City Hall, 125
city kid, 100

civic, 12
civil, 125
classic, 25
clear (roads), 12
climbing the walls, 198
clothespin, 89
clubs, 83
coal, 26
code, 158
coins, 35
cold snap, 198
colonies, 116
colonist, 116
color, 206
come on, 26, 108
commercial, 12
commuter, 140
compete, 166
complain, 140
conquered, 75
considered, 125
continent, 150
controversy, 150
cookout, 108
cool, 116
corned beef, 65
corn on the cob, 116
costumes, 75
couch, 140
country, 140
couples' spa day, 44
covered, 35
cowboys, 158
cozy, 219
crabs, 125
crack of dawn, 26
crafts, 35
craftspeople, 35
cranberry sauce, 166
cranky, 12
crazy, 201

crazy eights, 83
creamer, 217
crisp, 140
croaking, 100
crops, 166
cross your fingers, 12
crowd, 26
crowded, 26
crown, 125
cruise, 150
crunch, 100
crunchies, 26
crushed, 201
culprits, 26
cupcake, 100
cure, 56
cut a deck of cards, 83

D

date, 26, 125
day camp, 100
Daylight Saving Time, 56
day trip, 100
dead end, 140
dead of winter, 26
deal, 83
decade, 150
deck, 83
Declaration of Independence, 116
decorate, 26
decoration, 12
delivery boy, 200
department store, 125
designs, 12
dessert, 150
destination wedding, 125
destroy, 150
details, 125
diamonds, 83
dicey, 56

look out, 108
loose change, 57
loud, 36
lower, 116
loyalty, 126
lunar, 76
lunch box, 140
luv, 44

M

madly in love, 83
maid of honor, 126
make fun of, 150
make money, 116
make sure, 101
make your voice heard, 140
marchers, 66
marching bands, 150
Mardi Gras, 76
mariachi band, 89
marriage, 126
marshmallow, 44
mashed potatoes, 167
mask, 76
mayonnaise, 76
mayor, 13
maze, 140
mean, 27
medals, 140
melting pot, 126
menorah, 36
mention, 216
messy, 159
meteorologists, 13
middle of the night, 13
midnight, 13
minus (some number) degrees, 201
mirror, 66
miserable, 203
mistletoe, 27

mobbed, 27
modern, 126
molding, 210
monster, 159
moved; to be moved, 140
mow, 57
mug, 13
munch, 101
mwah, 44

N

nah, 208
nap, 13
national holiday, 108
native, 150
nativity, 27
naughty, 27
nearby, 27
needle, 27
newlyweds, 126
nightmare, 201
nighttime, 101
no kidding, 13
nothing to do, 44
no way, 203

O

oatmeal, 27
observance, 76
observe, 150
of course, 216
omelet, 76
onlookers, 76
only the strong survive, 150
on vacation, 101
ooh and aah, 116
orchard, 140
ornaments, 27
outdoors, 101

R

rainbow, 66
raining cats and dogs, 57
raise money, 13
rake, 140
rash, 203
raw, 76
reaction, 57
receipt, 27
reception, 126
recipe, 108
recite, 151
refreshments, 13
refund, 27
registry, 126
reindeer, 27
remembrance, 108
representative to Congress, 141
reservation, 44
resolutions, 13
response card, 126
resurrection, 76
returns, 27
reveal, 27
ribbon, 27
rich, 36
rides, 101
ring a bell, 57
ring in, 14
ring the doorbell, 200
rink, 201
Rockefeller Center, 201
rodent, 14
romantic, 44
route, 151
rude, 127
ruled, 117
run, 212
run out of (something), 159
rush hour, 141

S

sacrifice, 76
safe, 212
sails, 151
saint, 201
sales, 151
sandcastle, 101
saw, 83
saying, 108
scare, 141
scarecrows, 141
scary, 159
scenery, 44
scent, 141
school is out, 101
scoop, 76, 101
scrambled, 76
secret, 14
secular, 76
security, 141
seder, 76
senator, 141
served in the military, 108
set foot on, 151
set off, 14
set sail, 151
settle in, 27
seventh inning stretch, 212
shake hands 141
shamrock, 66
share, 127
sharpen, 141
shepherd, 27
shiver, 14
shocking, 27
shortcut, 151
shot, 218
shovel, 14
shower, 117
shuffle, 83
shy, 57

W

Y

Notes

Notes

Notes

Notes

Notes

Notes

_____
_____
_____
_____
_____
_____
_____
_____
_____
_____
_____
_____
_____
_____
_____
_____
_____
_____
_____
_____
_____
_____
_____
_____
_____

Notes

Notes

ENGLISH THE AMERICAN WAY®
Fun ESL Learning

The accent is on FUN in these friendly guides to language and culture in the U.S. Learn tons of new vocabulary. Improve your communication and pronunciation skills. Listen to short dialogues and read about interesting aspects of American culture. Learn wacky idioms, usage, and yes, some slang. Get great tips about social customs and everyday situations. Fun-filled quizzes and audio dialogues make it easy to practice, practice, practice until you're perfect!

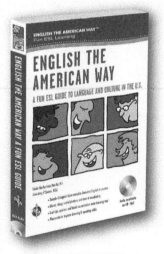

ISBN: 978-0-7386-0676-7

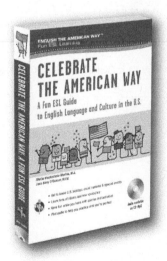

ISBN: 978-0-7386-1194-5

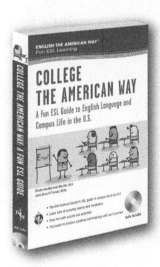

ISBN: 978-0-7386-1213-3

How to Use the Audio
Listen Everywhere!

CD—Listen to the audio CD at home, pop it into your car stereo, or play it on your computer at work. (Oops. Where's the boss?) The CD contains all the dialogues (Appendix A has each dialogue transcript and track number), so you can listen along as you read. It's a great tool to help you improve your own pronunciation.

Audio Download—Perfect for all your mobile devices. Head to *http://www.rea.com/etaw* for the audio content. After a quick download of the audio files (follow your media player's guide for instructions), you can hear all of the dialogues. Practice, practice, practice!

As you listen, pay special attention to the way the speakers . . . well, speak. You'll notice that words and phrases join together, rather than always being pronounced as separate sounds. Stop the audio as you listen, and try to copy the rhythm and stress of the speakers. You'll find that your own pronunciation will improve.

You know what we say in English: Practice makes perfect.

Have fun!